Women,
RISING

Women RISING

Amanda Antcliff

CREATION
HOUSE
A STRANG COMPANY

Women Rising by Amanda Antcliff
Published by Creation House
A Strang Company
600 Rinehart Road
Lake Mary, Florida 32746
www.strangbookgroup.com

Unless otherwise noted, all Scripture quotations are from the Holy Bible, New International Version of the Bible. Copyright © 1973, 1978, 1984, International Bible Society. Used by permission.

Scripture quotations marked AMP are from the Amplified Bible. Old Testament copyright © 1965, 1987 by the Zondervan Corporation. The Amplified New Testament copyright © 1954, 1958, 1987 by the Lockman Foundation. Used by permission.

Scripture quotations marked The Message are from The Message: The Bible in Contemporary English, copyright © 1993, 1994, 1995, 1996, 2000, 2001, 2002. Used by permission of NavPress Publishing Group.

All Greek and Hebrew definitions have been taken from the Blue Letter Bible online at www.blueletterbible.org.

All English definitions have been taken from the Microsoft Word dictionary tool.

Design Director: Bill Johnson
Cover design by Nathan Morgan

Library of Congress Control Number: 2009943068
International Standard Book Number: 978-1-61638-131-8

10 11 12 13 14 — 9 8 7 6 5 4 3 2 1
Printed in Canada

DEDICATION

I DEDICATE THIS BOOK TO YOU.
You were designed.
You were planned. You were created.
You are unique. You are precious. You are loved.
You are beautiful. You are God's daughter.
You are His masterpiece.

You love God.
You have desires. You have hopes.
You have talents. You have responsibilities. You have strengths.
You have potential. You have dreams.
You have purpose.

You have frustrations.
You have pain. You have insecurities.
You have doubt. You have discouragement. You have weakness.
You have pressures. You have challenges.
You have fears.

You have faith.
You are brave. You are strong.
You will grow. You will fight. You will win.
You will stand up. You will step out.
You will influence.

You are a woman rising!

I ALSO DEDICATE THIS BOOK TO MY HUSBAND, PATRICK.
You are my fellow adventurer in the journey of life.
I am who I am today because of your belief and encouragement.
You have always called me your "woman of God."
Thank you for helping me and allowing me to rise.
I am forever thankful.

CONTENTS

Foreword by Phil and Christine Pringle ix

Acknowledgments xi

Introduction: The Dream 1

PART ONE: ARISE, SHINE

1   The Call to Rise 7

2   The Call to Shine 23

3   Your Sphere of Influence 39

4   Why Must We Rise? 55

PART TWO: BOLDER, BRIGHTER LIGHTS

5   Lights Off or On; Dim or Bright? 79

6   Reclaiming Self 87

7   Confronting and Conquering Fear 109

8   Satan's Shackles 129

9   Demonic Opposition 145

10 God's Restraints 157

PART THREE: LIBERATING TRUTH

11 Truth Revealed 173

PART FOUR: STEPPING UP, STEPPING OUT

12 Preparing for Promotion 201

13 Ready, Set, Go 215

Final Words: I'm Cheering You On 229

Notes 233

About the Author 239

FOREWORD

We are living in exciting times. God is calling us to build churches that will impact our cities and nations with strong men and women working together as powerful teams. Amanda inspires women about God's plans and purposes and helps them identify their role in building the church and influencing their community.

I believe women are the heart of the church. They have the natural, beautiful ability to bring warmth, joy, and love to the house. In our church and movement, women are ministering, serving, and volunteering in hundreds of different roles, including leading churches, small groups, youth groups, and various departments within the church. Women are teaching in our colleges, leading the congregation in worship, pastoring our people, making decisions in board meetings, preaching from the pulpit, and interceding behind closed doors. Everywhere, women are rising to be leaders and pillars in the house of God. In my visits to the largest church in the world, Yoido Full Gospel Church in South Korea, I have seen firsthand the extraordinarily powerful effect of Dr. David Yonggi Cho having released thousands of women into leadership.

In this book, Amanda challenges women to overcome and fulfill their personal call so as to build the church and be a person of influence. Amanda is a gifted minister and a woman who loves God. Together with her husband, Patrick, they have faithfully served in our church team for over twenty years. They are involved in pastoring, teaching, leading our Bible college, and planting churches throughout Asia and Africa.

—Dr. Phil Pringle
President, C3 Church Global
Senior Minister, C3 Church, Sydney, Australia
Host of *Your Best Life with Phil Pringle*

Welcome, beautiful woman!

You are embarking on the journey of reading this book, which Amanda has written for *you*. The message in *Women Rising* captures what is stirring in my heart—the desire to see women growing, connected together, and rising to be strong pillars in the house of God. I have a clear vision in my heart that women's hands are anointed by God. These hands are filled with strength, compassion, healing, and love. These hands are working together, building the church, and reaching out to those around them. Amanda's words will help every woman discover and fulfill the unique and amazing work that God has prepared for her hands to perform.

This book is also about women enlarging their lives. Let me encourage you to take hold of the challenge that Amanda places before you: to pursue your dreams, express your creativity, start new businesses, reach out to strangers, and embark on new adventures.

I believe each of us can make a difference—in our marriages, in our families, in our friendships, in our churches, in our workplaces, in our schools, and in our communities. *Women Rising* will encourage you to make that difference. Without a doubt, this is the time and this is the season we will see the expanding influence of Christian women.

May you enjoy the journey of reading *Women Rising* and be encouraged and inspired by Amanda's life, her stories, and her insights. Happy reading.

—CHRISTINE PRINGLE
SENIOR MINISTER, C3 CHURCH, SYDNEY, AUSTRALIA

ACKNOWLEDGMENTS

MY FAMILY

- Thank you, Patrick, Jacinta, and Tyler, for your unending love, support, and belief in me.
- Thanks, Mum, for your encouragement throughout my life.

MY FRIENDS

- Thank you to my girlfriends who have cheered me on through the journey and adventure of writing this book.
- A big thanks to those special few who so graciously read my first manuscript.
- Thanks to my "pregnant" friends in Annie's group—you know who you are! The times and dreams we shared together will be treasured forever. You are now holding one of them.

MY WRITING COACH

- A special thanks to Merry Watson. You have so wisely led, guided, and supported me.

MY PUBLISHER

- Thank you to Brenda Davis and the team at Creation House for your support and skill in helping me share this message with others.

MY SPIRITUAL FAMILY

- Thanks, Pastors Phil and Chris Pringle, for your dedication to God and His house. Thank you for your input into my life and for the great example and inspiration you have been.
- Thank you to the other pastors in our church team and the C3 movement who have impacted my life.

MY GOD

- Thanks, God, for giving me life and freedom and for trusting me with this message and mission.

the dream

Introduction

THE DREAM

I believe in dreams.

I believe in the power of boldly declaring dreams.

The message of this book is my dream, but, more importantly, I believe it is God's dream.

This is the vision I see...

> I see women rising.
> I see women making a difference.
> I see women defying and defeating the devil.
> I see women living effective and successful lives.
> I see women forcefully advancing the kingdom of God.
> I see women released to express their gifts and their call.
> I see women pursuing their passions, potential, and purpose.
> I see women pushing through fear and growing in confidence.
> I see women building the church, making it bigger and stronger.
> I see women with unshackled feet standing up and stepping out.
> I see women whose lives are consecrated and committed to God.
> I see women carrying the presence and power of God into dark places.
> I see women partnering with men and influencing every area of society.

As you embark on the journey of reading this book, I would like both to welcome you and warn you. It is my belief that this book will change your life. You will read about God's dream for people, for the church, for cities, for nations, for His kingdom, and yes, even for your life. This will excite and inspire you, but I believe it will also challenge you. In order to write this book, I have had to live out this message. I have had to practice what I preach, so I know firsthand that the message of *Women Rising* will not only challenge you to grow but demand you to take action.

This book contains selected stories, revelations, and experiences from my twenty-five year walk of following and serving Jesus. *Women Rising*, though, was actually birthed in a single moment one bright, early spring morning when I had an encounter with God. I vividly remember being aroused from my sleep, and as I sat up in bed, God's presence invaded my room and my life. At that moment, the Holy Spirit planted this message into my heart, and I felt a strong burden and commission to write this book. Without any thought or hesitation, I wrote down the following words:

> *Write a prophetic mandate to my women.*
> *Tell them it is their time to rise; it is their time to shine.*

I continued to write:

> *My spirit is stirred with a burden to see women set free.*
> *Women whose hearts are unlocked,*
> *their eyes open to the vision and road set before them and*
> *their feet unshackled to run with the call of God.*
>
> *I see women soaring,*
> *running with arms outstretched and*
> *legs pumped with power and purpose.*
> *I see women rising,*
> *standing strong and living a life of influence.*
>
> *Today the King of kings and the Lord of lords is issuing*
> *a decree,*
> *a commission,*
> *a mandate.*
>
> *I hear His voice, and it is not softly spoken.*
> *He is speaking boldly and directly into our spirits.*
> *He is giving each of us a charge:*
> *"Arise, shine, and be a woman of influence."*

When God quickened these words to me I felt a very strong impression of the need to write this book and the need to do it *now*. I am so excited, because everywhere I turn, I hear a similar message. Women, it truly is our time. It is our time to rise, and it is our time to shine. It is our time to stand up, and it is our time to step out.

Women Rising deals with the mandate to rise and shine and why and how we are to influence. It addresses the reasons we have been hiding or have been covered; the personal issues that limit us; and the shackles that have been placed on women by other people, institutions, and cultures. It examines the biblical truth regarding the value, status, and roles of women and the character traits that must be evident in a woman's life if she is going to be promoted by God.

This book is about women rising, but it's not about a feminist uprising. My vision and my message is the promotion of partnership: men and women working side by side in marriages, ministry, and the marketplace. *Women Rising* is about women but has not been written only for women. I believe that the message and mandate of this book is also relevant to men, because we are all called to be people of influence. In addition to this, one of the themes of the book is that women will be released by others to fulfill their potential and purpose. Most men are in positions where they may empower or imprison women. It's my hope that men will choose to respect, raise, and release the women in their worlds. Therefore, *Women Rising* may benefit some men, either to strengthen what they are already doing or challenge them to embrace change.

As a life coach, Bible teacher, and pastor, I am passionate about empowering women, teaching the Scriptures, and building the church. Throughout this book I quote the Bible and prophetic words because I believe both are powerful and relevant. I value the truth of the Word of God because it provides understanding, builds faith, and brings freedom. I love knowledge and inspiration, but most importantly, that it is applied and acted upon, so each chapter concludes with questions in the Time to Reflect and Time to Act sections. For this reason, *Women Rising* is also a useful resource for women's Bible study groups.

The desire of my heart is that you will devour this book and catch its message. My prayer is that you will be freshly inspired by God's dream, and you will boldly stand up and step out to fulfill your part. My vision is that you will attain all He has purposed and destined for your life and that you will arise to become a woman of influence.

Are you ready?

Are you ready to be inspired about what God wants to do on planet Earth right now, to be stirred afresh with a mission from God, to be challenged about saving lost people, and to put up your hand to say yes to the King and His cause?

Are you ready to be empowered to step out and go for your dreams; to pursue your passions, purpose, and potential; and to face the issues in your life that are causing you to shrink back?

Are you ready to become a woman rising?

Yes? Then let's go.

arise, shine

Chapter One

THE CALL TO RISE

Throughout history there have been many women who have answered the call to rise. Four women in particular have inspired me, women whose lives left a mark on the planet. They were women who influenced others and made a difference. All of these women are now dead, but their lives still speak. Their courage to overcome fear calls me to be courageous. Their obedience to God summons me to be obedient. Their desire to serve others beckons me to serve. Their persistent faith stirs me to believe, and their decision to rise challenges me to stand up and step out. Let me tell you about my heroines.

Joan of Arc (1412–1431) was only thirteen when she began to see and hear God. In these prophetic visitations, a voice told her that she would liberate her homeland, France, from English domination. Boldly she approached the king and the leaders of the army with her mission. They tentatively appointed her captain of the army, yet her extraordinary leadership inspired men across the nation to take up arms and fight against the English, who had subjugated them for almost a century. At the age of seventeen, Joan clothed herself in a suit of armor and waving a banner with the image of our Savior brazenly led her troops into battle and glorious victory. This triumph paved the way for the coronation of King Charles VII of France. Shortly afterwards, Joan of Arc was sentenced to death for heresy and witchcraft, and at the age of nineteen she was burned at the stake. Only twenty-four years later her conviction was revoked, and Joan of Arc was named a martyr.[1]

My second heroine, Henrietta Mears (1890–1963), was a woman of vision and passion. She is remembered for the flamboyant hats and dresses she wore and the yellow-and-green car she drove, but mostly for her ability to transform people's lives. At the First Presbyterian Church in Hollywood, Henrietta taught the Bible to over four thousand young people. Throughout her life she led many to Christ, then challenged her disciples to serve Jesus and to dream big dreams.[2] She was instrumental in influencing the lives of two of the most gifted evangelists the world has ever known, Bill Bright and Billy Graham, thus playing a part in seeing billions of people across the world impacted with the gospel. Billy Graham said of her, "I doubt if any other woman outside my wife and mother has had such a marked influence on my life."[3]

Agnes Bojaxhiu (1910–1997) was only twelve years old when she made a decision to commit her life to serving God. At seventeen she became a nun in the order of the Sisters of Loretto and upon making her vows changed her name to Teresa. She heard a call from God to "help the poor while living among them." For over forty years this selfless woman devoted her life to caring for the needs of the hungry, the naked, the homeless, the crippled, the dying, the sick, the unwanted, and the unloved. She established the Missionaries of Charity in Calcutta, India, but her works spread throughout all of India and across the world. Her extraordinary faith, zeal, and compassion knew no boundaries. Today, her merciful spirit lives on. At the time of Mother Teresa's death, she had established approximately six hundred missions in one hundred and twenty countries, which included hospitals, orphanages, schools, homes, and hospices.[4]

My fourth heroine and history-maker is a woman from the Bible who lived three thousand years ago. Her name is Deborah.

THE STORY OF DEBORAH

Throughout the Old Testament we read of times when the nation of Israel obeyed God and times when they rebelled. During one of these rebellious periods, God handed Israel over to the control of its enemy. This meant that for many years the nation was cruelly oppressed under the reign of King Jabin of Canaan. It was during this dark period in Israel's history that God appointed Deborah, a prophetess, to be the judge and leader of the nation (Judges 3–5).

The Israelite people eventually realized that God could rescue them from the hand of their enemy, so they cried out to Him for help. God heard their prayers and brought deliverance through this mighty woman, Deborah. In a treacherous battle between the two nations, Deborah was instrumental in subduing King Jabin's army. This victory marked a turning point in Israel's history. In response to this wonderful conquest, Deborah sang a song. Here are some excerpts.

> *In the days of Shamgar son of Anath, in the days of Jael, the roads were abandoned; travelers took to winding paths. Village life in Israel ceased, ceased until I, Deborah, arose, arose a mother in Israel.... Then the people of the LORD went down to the city gates. "Wake up, wake up, Deborah! Wake up, wake up, break out in song!"*
> —JUDGES 5:6–7, 11–12

The oppression in Israel was so great that it had caused life to cease in the villages, and fear ruled the streets. There was no trade, no travel, and no tillage of the land. The whole nation of Israel was asleep, stagnant, and dead until Deborah chose to stand up and become a strong, godly leader. People everywhere were depending upon her so that life and peace could return to the nation. Deborah understood that God works through willing individuals; she chose to be willing, and she chose to rise.

GOD IS CALLING

One day on an airplane, I was doing some preparations to speak at a number of women's meetings. I prayed, "God what do you want me to say to the women? What is your message to them?" Immediately God quickened two passages of scripture to my heart. The words God spoke to me continue today to burn deep within my spirit, and they have become the foundational message of this book. These scriptures reflect the passion and the purpose of God; they speak of God's vision and mission for women all across the globe.

The first passage is Isaiah 60:1–3.

> *Arise, shine, for your light has come, and the glory of the LORD rises upon you. See, darkness covers the earth and thick darkness is over the peoples, but the LORD rises upon you and his glory appears over you. Nations will come to your light, and kings to the brightness of your dawn.*

God's desire is that women will rise and fulfill the potential and calling He has given them so that the glory of God will shine into dark places. These verses declare the very heartbeat of God. He loves hurting, lost, and oppressed people who are living in darkness, and He yearns for them to be set free by His glorious light. How will this happen? When we rise, shine, and become people of influence. Christians everywhere have a responsibility to bring light to their neighbors where they live; to their colleagues at their workplaces; or even, like Joan of Arc, to kings who rule over nations. This scripture encourages us that the level of our influence need have no limits.

The second passage is Matthew 5:14–16.

> *You are the light of the world. A city on a hill cannot be hidden. Neither do people light a lamp and put it under a bowl. Instead they put it on its stand, and it gives light to everyone in the house. In the same way, let your light shine before men, that they may see your good deeds and praise your Father in heaven.*

This scripture also talks about influence and our God-given position and command to be the light of the world. Through our good deeds and good lives we can influence others with the light, love, and power of God.

To *Arise*—What Does This Mean?

If God is calling His women to arise, then it is crucial that we understand what this word means and what we must do. After a thorough search of many dictionaries and thesauruses I have summarized the words *arise* and *rise* into four definitions.

Definition 1: To *Arise* means "to get up or stand up"

Arise is a verb, which means it is a word of action. When we arise, we move our bodies into a different position. We cannot arise and stay the same. For example, the term *arise* often applies to getting out of bed or getting out of a chair. In both cases, we are no longer in a stationary or sedentary position. When we arise we stand and get ready to take steps and take action. The process of arising also affects our physique and posture; we appear taller and larger. In summary, when we arise, we grow to the fullness of our stature.

I love the two images in Matthew 5:14–16, which vividly capture what it means to be the light of the world. The first is a city on a hill that cannot be hidden and the second is a light on a stand that brings light to everyone in the house. I believe both of these pictures reflect the vision God has of His women that we are:

strong

confident

upright

bold

radiant

effective

important

elevated

prominent

influential

To arise, then, is a decision that we make to:

stand up in stature and step out to influence.

I want you to take hold of this statement, because it encapsulates what God is dreaming and believing for His daughters. He sees:

- **Who we are:** As women of stature we are distinctive, bold, beautiful, imposing, confident, and strong.
- **What we can do:** As women of stature we are important and influential, significant and successful.
- **How others regard us:** As women of stature we are highly respected and esteemed by others.

Definition 2: To *Arise* means "to develop, evolve, grow, or build"

Arising is both a journey and a process. God calls us to arise throughout our whole lives. It is not a one-shot incident or decision but a continual transformation. You may have just read the list of adjectives I used to describe the light on the stand and the city on a hill and said to yourself, "I'm a long way off from having these qualities in my life. Me, strong? No! Me, confident? No! Me, influential? No!" Like you, I am also on this journey. However, instead of feeling overwhelmed by how far I have to go, I allow the images presented in this scripture to inspire and compel me to grow and to keep rising.

I love flowers and the word *bloom*. I believe, as we choose to walk the journey of rising, we bloom like a beautiful flower. This is highlighted in 2 Corinthians 3:18, "And we, who with unveiled faces all reflect the Lord's glory, are being transformed into his likeness with ever-increasing glory, which comes from the Lord, who is the Spirit." A wise woman makes a commitment to grow to the fullness of her stature. Every day she can have a little more glory and light shining from within her. This verse is an inspiration and a vision for my life.

> *The path of the righteous is like the first gleam of dawn, shining ever brighter till the full light of day.*
> —PROVERBS 4:18

Definition 3: To *Arise* means "to rebel or revolt"

During revolutions people arise and stand up to authorities that have kept them imprisoned or in bondage. It is my belief that there are many factors that have contributed to women being confined and restrained. In the passage from Matthew 5:14–16, we read that some lights have been hidden or concealed because they have been placed under bowls, thus rendering the light ineffective. Unfortunately, it is the same in the lives of many women across the globe. We need to ask the question, What are the authorities that have constrained women and bound their hands, feet, and mouth?

Firstly, and most significantly, we have kept ourselves hidden through our own insecurities and fears. Secondly, cultures, institutions, and other people have kept us shackled. Some have done this unintentionally, while others have instituted laws and customs that are anti-women. Thirdly, I believe Satan does not like women, especially women who rise and make a mark on this earth.

We will talk more about each of these matters later in the book. However, let me say for now that if women are going to rise, then we must take resolute and decisive action against the different forces that attempt to imprison and oppose us. Revolution starts within you and within me. Let's overcome personal fears and limitations. Let's recognize who and what we are hiding behind. Let's rise up and overcome intimidation. Let's pray and break demonic resistance. Let's:

stand out and be different and
stand up and make a difference.

Definition 4: To *Arise* means "to become active or vocal"

I believe as women arise they will find their feet, hands, and voice. Many women have been brought up in environments where they have not been free to express their opinions, talents, or call. This has radically changed over the last century, but many women are still limited and hindered in their marriages, families, churches, communities, and nations.

I'm of the opinion that many women's mouths have been gagged, their voices silenced and suppressed. To have a voice means:

- the right to be heard, to speak, to vote;
- to express an opinion or view; and
- to influence.

When we have a voice we have the power to lead, to create new ideas and directions, and to bring change and influence. I sense we are in a time when restraints are being removed and women's mouths are being opened and anointed by God to speak, not only for themselves but also on His behalf. Like my four heroines, I believe more women's voices will be used to bring wisdom, truth, freedom, and justice.

I believe many women have experienced upper limits of the opportunities and positions to which they have been able to rise. Possibly, this is even happening to you. But let me encourage you that in God there is no ceiling. Women can attain any position within the church, their career, and the community. We have to trust that if God has chosen and called us, then He will make a way, even when it seems impossible.

We are in a new era of God anointing women to rise to influential and prominent positions. Christian women will teach, preach, and govern within the church and hold important positions in every field within our communities, businesses, and governments.

When We Arise ... God Arises

In Isaiah 60:1–3 we are encouraged only once to "arise," but twice it is declared that "the Lord rises upon you." As we arise, so does God. And when God arises, so does His glory. God's glory is His splendor, power, and authority. It's this glory that will overshadow us and bring favor upon our lives. It's God's glory in us that will affect others and cause us to be people of influence.

When we rise up, we become more the person God has destined and purposed us to be. Our potential is unlocked, and the fullness of our call is realized. We are changed individuals with the capacity to bring change into other people's lives. This brings a smile on God's face and delight to His heart.

How wonderful is this verse from Song of Solomon, "My lover spoke and said to me, 'Arise, my darling, my beautiful one, and come with me'" (Song of Sol. 2:10). How gentle Jesus is. Jesus is calling you and me to arise and to come. As He gently but persuasively beckons, we can be assured that He will lead the way and walk with us hand in hand on our journey. I believe we can't say no to Jesus, who is summoning us to arise and to come.

My Story

Each of my four heroines made a choice to arise, and their decision brought salvation and freedom to others.

I often think of Deborah and ask myself the questions, Who needs me to awaken and arise? Who is lost, lonely, and lifeless and calling out for me to rise and deliver them? At times I have the inescapable impression that on the other side of my obedience to what God is asking me to do—on the other side of being challenged and stretched—there are people waiting for me to touch them, inspire them, teach them, and deliver them.

A very significant year for me was 1998. It was a year when I received many prophecies, and God gave me visions of what He was calling me to do in my future. The word and the dream He placed into my life that year were far bigger than me. I was small in every respect: in confidence, faith, skill, character, experience, authority, knowledge, capacity, and anointing. I have discovered that with enlarged vision comes a process of enlarging self. The vision is always bigger than who we are at that time. For the vision to be fulfilled, we have to grow and rise in many areas of our life. This is the reason a lapse of time occurs between the conception of a dream and its completion.

Shortly after my encounters in 1998, God started to speak very clearly into my spirit these two words:

RISE UP

I have to write these words in big, bold letters because that is how I felt them in my spirit: very strong and very loud. For many months during worship in our church services, all I could hear were the words *rise up*.

At times I thought I would burst. There were moments when I felt as if God was punching me on the inside. At other times I worshiped with my arms outstretched, as high and as far as they could reach. I knew God was taking me through an intensive operation of enlargement. I have since discovered on the different occasions when I have ministered that many other women have also experienced this call to rise up.

Over the years, I have had to apply "rise up" to a number of areas of my life. I want to share these with you as an example, because I know that God will also call you to grow and to rise. My hope is that my experiences may inspire and help you through your own process and journey.

Rise as a Preacher

My first call by God was to rise as a preacher. This was an area of ministry that was totally new to me. It was both exciting and scary. God had given me a vision of myself preaching to audiences and ministering the Holy Spirit to people during altar calls. I had taught in classrooms, ran small groups, and had even spoken at youth groups; but I never preached from a pulpit in church services or at conferences. For me to rise as a preacher, I had to learn many things and overcome many fears.

One day God said these words to me:

"Amanda, you prepare yourself; I will prepare your way."

From this instruction I understood that the dream He had given me was in His hands and that I did not have to push open any doors to make it happen. He would prepare my way. There was one condition, however: I had to prepare myself. I had to do my part. This meant taking actions that would equip me to do this new thing that God was calling me to do. These were the practicalities of rising up.

So, I enrolled in my husband's preaching course at the Bible college where I was already a lecturer teaching other subjects. To pass the course, I was required to preach to my own students, who were now my fellow classmates. This was very unnerving. When I preached my mouth was dry, and I spoke too fast. However, I felt victorious that day because I had pushed through and conquered many fears.

I also intently observed other preachers. On one occasion I traveled interstate to see Cindy Jacobs preach at a women's conference. I had read her books but desperately wanted to see her in person. I was inspired by her boldness. This trip was also significant for me because I had spent years raising my two children and had not traveled on my own for a long time. I had lost my confidence. The cure for my apprehension was to actually do it, and to do it on my own. I also felt prompted to take further steps of preparation. I bought some new clothes that would be suitable to wear when preaching, and I joined a group of women who ministered from the pulpit. With these ladies I shared my dreams, and they nurtured, enriched, and challenged me.

Eventually there came a time when God did provide opportunities to preach in other churches and conferences, both in Australia and internationally. What an amazing adventure it has been! I love being able to carry and deliver a message from God and see people's lives changed. Some of my dreams have not yet come to pass. I am still in days of preparation and will continue to be on a journey of rising in this area for many years ahead.

Rise as a Leader

In my Christian walk, I have come to realize that though you may be a preacher, a pastor, and a teacher, operating in these roles does not necessarily make you a leader. One day it suddenly dawned on me that, despite being a minister, I was actually not an effective leader. For most of my married life I have taken on leadership responsibilities together with my husband, but I have to admit that for the first fifteen years of our marriage I allowed him to do most of the leading. I lacked the confidence and even the willingness to take charge and to grow in this area. I felt very comfortable working under his guidance and authority. If we had leadership meetings in our home, I would hide behind him and my hospitality role.

A number of years ago our church pastoral system changed, and we were encouraged to run same-sex small groups. Up until then Pat and I had been running two small groups together in our home. They were mixed groups, and Pat was the leader of them both.

With this change of focus God issued a personal challenge to me. Would I rise as a leader and take on the running of my own groups, or would I remain limited and hidden? To be honest, I didn't want to become a leader because I understood what it would entail: increased responsibility, personal enlargement, and the need for greater capacity. There was, however, a cry in my spirit to rise and be all that I could be. I also knew that many women are yearning and searching to have mentors or role models to follow. I wanted to be that for women, and I knew if I arose, so would others. So, I took up the challenge and began leading two female small groups and my own pastoral network.

Rise as a Businesswoman

I am passionate about the Proverbs 31 woman. For many years I have aspired to be everything she is: a great wife, a loving mother, an organized household manager, an influential elder in the community, a lover of God, a helper of the poor. There came a time when God began calling me to be, like her, a businesswoman.

The Proverbs 31 woman's passions were sewing and spinning, and with these talents she established a successful business as a clothes merchant.

The money she earned was then wisely invested into property and a vineyard. In the words of author Elizabeth George, "She developed something personal into something professional."[5] This was my inspiration!

I decided to take my "personal" and make it into "something professional." My talents are teaching practical truths and pastoring people, so in 2006 I launched my life coaching business, Your Café Coach. In quiet cafes, homes, offices, over the phone, or Internet, I connect with people and help them progress in all different areas of their lives. I love being "Coach Amanda" because I have the opportunity to encourage, support, guide, and empower people to live more satisfying and successful lives. The journey of establishing my business has been and continues to be a significant call to personally rise.

One thing that burns in my heart is the knowledge that God is calling some women to rise in the business and professional world. God needs strong Christian women to be an influence in every sphere of society and, in particular, to have a voice in the marketplace. I know that many women carry the seed for a business inside them. I hope my example will encourage you to keep dreaming and stepping out to see that seed grow into a prosperous business. Let me ask you this question, What is your personal that you could turn professional?

Rise as a Worker of the Harvest

Throughout my late twenties and for most of my thirties, my life was focused on church and ministry. My husband was working full-time in the church, my children were attending our church school, and my friends were all from church. One day I realized our family was suffocating in a sea of smallness. I think God was feeling it too, because He began to shift our hearts, our eyes, and our lives to see and touch the lost.

Since that wake-up call, my family and I have risen as workers of the harvest. We have felt a fresh commissioning to *go* that has required us to stand up and step out. We have positioned ourselves to reach out to others in our community who are living in darkness without Jesus in their life. Starting my business was one of these steps, since some of my clients are non-believers. We also moved our children to the school in our own suburb, and we joined our local sporting clubs.

What changed most, however, was my attitude to witnessing. Previously I dreaded sharing my faith with other people. I always felt embarrassed, awkward, and motivated by guilt. But something changed, and it became easy. God showed me new, simple strategies: remember people's names, stop and have a chat, invite people to my home, or do a simple act of kindness.

I came to realize that first and foremost I needed to win people to myself before they would be won to Jesus. I love what international evangelist Christine Caine said at a conference I attended: "No longer must we *do* witnessing; we must *be* a witness."[6]

> *Do you not say, "Four months more and then the harvest"? I tell you, open your eyes and look at the fields! They are ripe for harvest.*
>
> —JOHN 4:35

This scripture says the harvest is ripe. Therefore, we must be ready and prepared to reap it. We must live with a conviction of our responsibility and our mission. Live with our eyes open to see lost people. Live with feet eager to walk through doors of opportunity. Live with our hands ready to reach out and help. Live with a willingness to act, even when it is neither comfortable nor convenient. Live with a heart open to be engaged in the lives of others.

Let me share with you a very important thing I have learned: God yearns for the whole world to be saved, but I can't do that. Neither can you. But together we can. All you and I have to do is play our parts. We only need to know and touch those whom God has given us personally to reach. Even Jesus, when He lived on Earth, knew that He was not called to minister to everyone. Our mission, our responsibility, and ultimately our choice is to do what Jesus did.

> *I have revealed you to those whom you gave me out of the world. They were yours; you gave them to me and they have obeyed your word....I pray for them. I am not praying for the world, but for those you have given me, for they are yours.*
>
> —JOHN 17:6, 9

I have shared with you the four different areas in my life in which God has called me to rise. I am certain that He is also whispering (or shouting!) into your ear the same words He spoke to me: "Rise up."

Are you willing, like Deborah, to take up the challenge? I am so excited about who and what is waiting on the other side of you rising up. It is my belief that we each have the potential to be heroines and history makers. Every one of us can choose to be strong and courageous women who are ready and willing to impact this world for God. Will you?

There is in this world no such force as the force of a [wo]man determined to rise.

—W. E. B. DuBois (1868–1963)[7]
CIVIL RIGHTS ACTIVIST AND AUTHOR

TIME TO REFLECT

- What women (dead or alive) have inspired your life? Why?
- How could you be a heroine or a history maker?
- In what areas in your life do you need to:
    Get up or stand up?
    Develop, evolve, grow, or build?
    Rebel or revolt?
    Become active or vocal?
- Up until now, what or who has stopped you from rising?

TIME TO ACT

- Decide upon one thing you can put into action this week that will force you to rise in some area of your life.
- Apply this statement to yourself:
    "_____ (insert your name), you prepare yourself, and I will prepare your way."

Chapter Two

THE CALL TO SHINE

The call to rise is a summons to be a person of influence.

The call to shine concerns how we can influence.

One day I was at a ladies' meeting where one woman made this perceptive comment:

We are not all called to be leaders but we are all called to influence.

What a great statement! I totally agree that we all have the ability to be influential women. In fact, we will actually be an influence whether we consciously choose to be or not. Everything we are and everything we do has the potential to influence ourselves, others, or our environment. Every word we speak, every decision we make, every attitude we embrace, every emotion we feel, and every action we take can have a positive or negative influence. The important thing to remember is that we have the potential, the power, and the choice to be an influential person who can bring good rather than harm.

To influence means "to be able to impact, affect, change, sway, or shape something or somebody." We can do this for good through love, compassion, encouragement, leadership, motivation, inspiration, or even fighting for a cause. We can also influence in a negative way through manipulation, disinterest, abuse, condemnation, aggression, or sarcasm. How we affect the people or situations that surround us is our choice.

Put simply, to be a woman of influence means making a positive difference by impacting lives or bringing about change. As women of God we must not seek influence for our own pride, power, or prestige. Our influence should always be for the expansion of His name, His glory, and His kingdom.

HOW CAN WE INFLUENCE?

The Bible uses many words and images to describe the different ways Christians can influence. Each of these is inspiring and insightful when it comes to understanding who we are and what we are called to do. We are:

- Ministers: We are fashioned to serve others.
- God's Ambassadors: We represent God here on Earth (2 Cor. 5:20).
- Ministers of Reconciliation: We connect people to God (2 Cor. 5:18).
- Priests: We stand between God and people (1 Pet. 2:9).
- Salt: We bring flavor to the world (Matt. 5:13).
- Part of the Body: We have a gift and a role to perform in the church (1 Cor. 12).
- His Workmanship: We are created to do good works (Eph. 2:10).
- A Fragrant Aroma: We are the scent of Jesus on Earth (2 Cor. 2:14–15).
- Fishers of Men: We are to bring people to Jesus (Matt. 4:19).

In this chapter, we are going to focus on five other metaphors that powerfully capture the different ways Christians can be influential. These images specifically relate to the message of this book and the theme of women rising.

1. WE ARE LIGHT

Jesus proclaimed these two truths:

"I am the light of the world."

—JOHN 8:12

"You are the light of the world."

—MATTHEW 5:14

It's good to be reminded that as Christians we are called a light because we have Jesus living inside us, and it is His light which shines from our lives.

Jesus' light is so bright, pure, and beautiful that in heaven there will be no night and no need for additional light sources.

> *The city does not need the sun or the moon to shine on it, for the glory of God gives it light, and the Lamb is its lamp.*
>
> —Revelation 21:23

Wherever Jesus' light shines there is no darkness and there is no death. Jesus described Himself as "the light of life" (John 8:12). As carriers of Jesus' light, we too can transmit this life in all its fullness and power.

Where there is light there is love, freedom, healing, forgiveness, righteousness, salvation, peace, joy, mercy, justice, truth, and everything else that Christ embodies. Where there is darkness, God is absent and Satan rules. In the dark there is pain, confusion, loneliness, despair, hopelessness, and sin. People are either living in the light or living in the darkness. As Christians, our commission and responsibility is the same as the apostle Paul: "I am sending you to them to open their eyes and turn them from darkness to light, and from the power of Satan to God" (Acts 26:17–18).

> *Arise, shine, for your light has come, and the glory of the LORD rises upon you. See, darkness covers the earth and thick darkness is over the peoples, but the LORD rises upon you and his glory appears over you. Nations will come to your light, and kings to the brightness of your dawn.*

This is our key passage of scripture, from Isaiah 60:1–3. Take a moment to reread it. Notice afresh the extent of the darkness that covers the lives of individuals, families, people groups, communities, rulers, cities, and nations. The adjective used to describe the darkness is *thick*. That means it is broad, wide, deep, and dense. This darkness is the reason for the desperation, deception, and depravity in the world today. It is this darkness that separates people from God. But look at the amazing effect of the light when it shines in the dark. It attracts and draws others toward its radiant power and brightness.

I love these words of King David:

You are my lamp, O Lord; the Lord turns my darkness into light.
—2 Samuel 22:29

As lights of the world, our role is to bring Jesus into dark lives and dark places. We have the ability to help others, like King David, turn from darkness to light. The greatest influence we can have in someone else's life is to introduce them to Jesus. Our light can help others to see the Truth, the Way, and the Life.

As lights, we also have the responsibility to carry the heart and mind of Jesus into this world. Wherever God has strategically placed us, we can be His representative. As Christians we should be the ones to radiate exemplary character, attitudes, and behavior.

We can also shine by what we contribute. I believe Christians can access God's genius, wisdom, and knowledge. Therefore, we can be the people in the workplace who come up with the creative ideas, inventions, scientific discoveries, technological advancements, revolutionary concepts, breakthrough strategies, highest sales, and best performances. It is in this pragmatic but powerful way that our lives can shine and bring glory to God.

2. We Are Mothers

In the previous chapter I referred to the story of Deborah. I absolutely love a term that Deborah used to describe herself. She said, "I...arose a mother" (Judg. 5:7). Not only was she a judge, a leader, and a prophetess, but she became a mother to the whole nation of Israel. She carried these people in her heart and fought for them as only a mother would fight for her natural children. I believe this concept of mothering beautifully captures the qualities of a feminine leader.

- **A mother is a life giver.** She has the ability to conceive, carry, and give birth.
- **A mother is a nurturer.** She can love, nourish, care, protect, and feed her precious ones.
- **A mother is a disciplinarian.** She must train, instruct, set boundaries, and admonish her children.

- **A mother is a role model**. She must disciple, encourage, empower, believe in, and lead those under her care.

Any woman of any age can be a mother. You can be a spiritual mom even when you are not a natural mom. Neither do our spiritual children have to be younger than we are; we can mother people our own age or even those who are older than us. I believe God is calling more women to rise as mothers because there are so many people who are crying out in our churches and communities to be nurtured, raised, and led by loving, godly women. Let me ask you today, Will you be a woman who will embrace and empower others?

When I returned to Jesus in my late teens, one of my first roles serving Him was to lead a small group of girls. I met with these girls every week for four years and traveled with them through most of their high school years. Even though I was both young in age and spiritual maturity, I mothered these girls because I cared for them and loved them. I instructed them, believed in them, supported them, and was an example for them to follow. As women we can be spiritual moms in our workplaces, in our neighborhoods, at our churches, and in our extended families.

I am inspired by Paul's words to Timothy, his son in the faith:

> I have been reminded of your sincere faith, which first lived in your grandmother Lois and in your mother Eunice and, I am persuaded, now lives in you also....But as for you, continue in what you have learned and have become convinced of, because you know those from whom you learned it, and how from infancy you have known the holy Scriptures.
>
> —2 TIMOTHY 1:5; 3:14–15

Timothy was a godly young man due in part to the profound influence of two amazing women in his life: his mother and his grandmother. From these women he received two things: a love for the Word and a spirit of faith. I believe when we mother, we can actually impart the spirit which is inside us to those who place themselves under our care and our covering. The qualities or spiritual gifts we have are transferrable. They are able to be "caught" or given away. For example, if we are bold, our "children" can be bold. If we are wise, they too can be wise. If we move in certain spiritual gifts, these also can be passed on to our children.

Being a mother is such an extraordinary privilege and blessing. We have been entrusted by God with the divine responsibility to lead and love our children. As mothers, we have the power to encourage and enable our biological or spiritual children to believe in themselves. Through care and guidance we can influence our children to rise and stand tall. There is no greater joy than helping a child mature to become strong and secure and to fulfill their potential and purpose.

3. WE ARE BUILDERS

The wise woman builds her house, but with her own hands the foolish one tears hers down.

—PROVERBS 14:1

The Book of Proverbs has a wonderful way of using striking imagery to highlight extremes. This scripture depicts two influential women at opposite ends of the spectrum: the wise woman who builds her house, and the foolish woman who tears hers down. Both women are bringing influence—one for good, the other for harm.

Reckless words pierce like a sword, but the tongue of the wise brings healing.

—PROVERBS 12:18

The tongue has the power of life and death.

—PROVERBS 18:21

Women have in their hands and their mouths the power to build up or to tear down. We can have a profound impact in the lives of those we regularly spend time with, such as our husbands, children, friends, and work colleagues. We can also build the environment and atmosphere at the places we live and work with our words, attitudes, emotions, characters, and spirits.

The term *builder* is rich with meaning. It encompasses the multifaceted roles of designer, engineer, and laborer. As women we can use all of these abilities to benefit the lives of others, our homes, our workplaces, and our communities. We have the ability to conceive and create, to plan and strategize, to construct and decorate. As builders, we are involved in every part of the process.

> *By wisdom a house is built, and through understanding it is established; through knowledge its rooms are filled with rare and beautiful treasures.*
>
> —PROVERBS 24:3–4

When I read this scripture it brings to mind the amazing palaces in Europe I visited when I was twelve years old. They were truly magnificent. Each room, hallway, and ceiling was filled with precious furniture, paintings, and decorations. As a builder I can create this same grandeur and glory in the people and places in my life. It is my desire to build greatness in my marriage, my children, my home, my business, my ministry, and every other area of my life.

4. WE ARE PILLARS

Our daughters will be like pillars carved to adorn a palace.
—PSALM 144:12

Women are pillars! I love this image. Notice that we are not just any old, ordinary concrete pillars hiding away in some insignificant building. Rather, we are majestic pillars that have been carved to ornament the king's palace. Yet as pillars, we are much more than a mere decorative feature, because we also have a fundamental power and purpose.

During my travels I have seen many different styles and shapes of pillars, but when I think of women as pillars, I think of the *Porch of the Maidens* in the Erechtheion temple at Athens. The extraordinary feature of this temple is the six female statues that are actually pillars supporting the roof over the porch. These sculptured women are truly beautiful, and each one is uniquely different.

If women are pillars, then it's important for us to have an understanding of the role and purpose of this architectural feature. A pillar is "a vertical column that is part of a building or structure, and it can either be a support or a decoration."[1] A pillar is normally free-standing, tall, and slender. The main function of a pillar is to provide support for something heavy, such as an overhang, beam, or ceiling. Pillars, therefore, must be strong, able to bear and carry weight. Their role is to keep structures firm and steadfast, preventing them from collapsing or breaking.

I believe this image of women as pillars is a metaphor encouraging and calling women to rise as leaders. Women who aspire to leadership positions must make the choice to stand tall and be strong and self-assured. They must take up the role of supporting others and shouldering the weight of responsibility. If we are going to be pillars and leaders, then we must be women who are capable, responsible, and dependable.

Many of us are pillars in our families, workplaces, and churches. We have others relying on us to take up our authority and take hold of responsibility. It is important that as pillars we are women who remain upright, strong, and secure so that we are able to carry this weight of leadership. If we fall apart or become weak, it can trigger a domino effect of collapse around us. If we want our leadership to strengthen, we must keep growing in our character and our capacity. The greater our strength, the greater the weight we are able to carry.

A pillar is elegant and beautiful. To me, this means that our leadership as women must always be feminine. We must lead as women. I love this comment about the maiden pillars in the Erechtheion temple: "They are engineered in such a way that their slenderest part, the neck, is capable of supporting the weight of the porch roof whilst remaining graceful and feminine."[2]

Many years ago I tore a page from a magazine that featured an advertisement from Wedgwood, a famous English company that manufactures fine bone china. There was a photograph of an exquisitely designed dinner plate, and the caption read, "Like a ballerina, you see the beauty and not the remarkable strength." The copy went on, "Looking at a piece of Wedgwood fine bone china, most people assume it is fragile and meant for special occasions. In reality, Wedgwood china possesses remarkable strength…It is the perfect combination of beauty and strength, so you really can enjoy it every day."[3] This reminds me of the qualities of the Proverbs 31 woman, who was a remarkable pillar in her home, the community, and marketplace. The Bible describes her as a leader and a lady who was "clothed with strength and dignity" (Prov. 31:25).

The pillars described in Psalm 144:12 adorn the palace, which is the home of the king. I believe the palace is symbolic of the church, since this is where Jesus, the King of kings, abides. For many centuries the role of women in the church was weak and minimal. In most places women have not been allowed to be pillars or leaders. In the 1900s we saw some amazing women rise and do great things for God, people like Aimee Semple McPherson and Kathryn Kuhlman. However, I believe we are in the times when God is not just calling the ones or twos but the thousands. Now is the time when women can rise to be ministers and leaders in the house of God.

A number of years ago I had the privilege of listening to David (née Paul) Yonggi Cho, the pastor of the world's largest church, Yoido Full Gospel Central Church in Seoul, South Korea. I vividly remember a story he shared about how he prayed to God for a strategy on how to grow and pastor his church. The solution that came to him was to start a "cell" system with small groups meeting in people's homes.

Dr. Cho invited the men in his congregation to lead these cell groups, but many of them politely refused. As a consequence, Dr. Cho turned to the women, focusing on raising and releasing them to be effective leaders in his church. Today, the strength of this extraordinary church is its cell groups, and most of these are run by women—thousands upon thousands of them. Two-thirds of his ordained pastors are women. What David Yonggi Cho did was controversial and revolutionary. Up until that point women had a subordinate role, and his decision marked a major paradigm shift both in the church and in the Korean culture.

One night my husband had a dream: He was with his peers in ministry at an army camp close to the battlefield. They were being deployed by the commander to take troops to the front line and fight the enemy. The commander sent Pat to a tent that had a sign over the door that read "Officer

Training." When he walked into the room, he noticed that many of the soldiers being trained to become officers were women.

It is important to highlight that in the armed forces the rank of officer is a position of leadership. On the U.S. Army Web site the responsibilities and qualities of a commissioned officer are described:

> *Commissioned Officers are the leaders of the Army. They lead Soldiers during every aspect of a mission. Commissioned Officers are also supporters and problem solvers. They make decisions quickly, always focusing on completing the mission successfully and showing respect for their subordinates. Commissioned Officers lead from the front and adjust to environments that are always changing. To be a Commissioned Officer is to be respected as a Soldier, an inspiring leader and a servant of the nation. In addition to exhibiting self-discipline, initiative, confidence and intelligence, Commissioned Officers are physically fit and can perform under physical and mental pressures. They are judged by their ability to make decisions on their own and bear ultimate moral responsibility for those decisions.*[4]

I find this description of the roles and attributes of an officer both inspiring and challenging. Leadership is a position, but it is also a quality that you and I can continually develop in our lives. Like the pillar, we can choose to be carved by the hand of God and be strengthened in our ability and capacity to be a leader.

5. We Are Hands

My pastor, Christine Pringle, relayed a vision she had for the women in our church. She saw a pair of hands stretched out. The ten fingers were growing, and they had no end. It was a picture that portrayed the different roles and influence that women could have both in our church and in the communities in which they lived. The growing, endless fingers represented women being released and their influence having no boundary or limit.

This vision excited me, because I saw it as a vision for women, symbolizing what we can do and how we can be an influence. I decided to do a Bible study on the word *hands* and discovered that there are ten main functions that hands perform. These might symbolize the different areas in which women can be an influence. These ten roles appear in the table on page 34, each with two scripture references, together with a number of examples of how this role might function within the church and the community. As you read these diverse examples, I would encourage you to identify which function of the hand you are more likely to perform.

At times you will probably find your hands performing several of these ten functions, because most of these roles are universal Christian responsibilities. For example, everyone can lift their hands in worship and prayer, and we can all use our hands to work. At times each of us will need to fight, and every believer can lay hands on the sick and see the power of God move. I strongly believe, however, that you are more likely to find yourself doing one or, at the most, two of the roles listed in the table with greater passion, ease, and frequency than the others.

I get excited about this list of roles because it is so broad and diverse. Women can be used in any and every place and position in the church and society, depending on their unique gifts and call. I love this scripture: "Whatever your hand finds to do, do it with all your might" (Eccles. 9:10). Let this word of God be an inspiration to you. Whatever you are good at, make sure you are doing it with pleasure, passion, and pizzazz.

In this chapter we have studied five metaphors that beautifully and powerfully portray the influence we can have as women. We are lights, mothers, builders, pillars, and hands. In the next chapter we will seek to more precisely define who, where, and how you can influence. I believe it's absolutely crucial to know your specific sphere of influence.

	Role: Hands that–	Scriptures	Function in Church	Function in Community
1	Worship and Praise	Neh. 8:6 Ps. 47:1	Worship, music, and dance teams	Bands or dance groups that perform and impact beyond the church
2	Pray	2 Chron. 6:12–13 1 Tim. 2:8	Intercession and prayer teams	Prayer groups in our communities (e.g., schools, workplaces, hospitals, parliament)
3	Work	Neh. 4:16–18 Prov. 31:13, 19	Volunteer teams, deacons, church staff (e.g. hospitality, organizing events, welcome desk, bookshop, cleaning, community programs, receptionist, accounts, administration)	Professions in the business world, such as banking, accounting, retail, event management, research, service, and sales industries; trades such as chefs, firefighters, plumbers, electricians, and gardeners
4	Build and Create	Prov. 14:1–2 2 Chron. 2:1–2,7	Technical, creative, and practical help teams (e.g., sound, lighting, graphics, computer, drama, art, multimedia, building and equipment maintenance)	Professions in the artistic, creative, technical, beauty, advertising, fashion, entertainment, engineering, and building industries
5	Love, Help and Give	Proverbs 31:20 Luke 10:30-35	Counselling, pastoral and practical helps teams. Entrepreneurial women who give finances.	Professions in medicine, nursing, health areas, counselling and social work.
6	Guide	Ps.139:10; 23:3	Cell/small groups, pastoral, teaching, preaching, and leading different ministries (e.g., new Christians, children, youth, men, women)	Professions in teaching, training, coaching, mentoring, and counseling
7	Fight and Proclaim Victory	Exod. 17:11–13 Neh. 4:17	Apostles, pastors, and intercessors	Politicians, lawyers, police, activists in social justice areas, armed forces
8	Bless, Equip and Release	Acts 6:6 1 Tim. 4:14	Apostles, pastors, teachers, prophets, leaders, and preachers	CEOs, managers, and departmental heads
9	Transfer God's Power	Luke 4:40 Acts 8:17–18	Apostles, pastors, evangelists, prophets, leaders, and preachers	Any person who is seeing the miraculous occurring outside the church context
10	Lead and Govern	Judg. 7:7–9, Ps. 8:6; 78:72	Apostles, pastors, elders, church board members, department leaders, and general managers	Politicians, CEOs, principals of education institutions, department heads

TIME TO REFLECT

- How do you respond to the statement, "We are all called to influence"?
- Identify examples from your everyday life of when you influence in positive and negative ways. What is the effect of your influence?
- What does it mean to you to be described as a:
  Light
  Mother
  Builder
  Pillar
  Hand

TIME TO ACT

- What are some practical ways you can increase the level of influence in your relationships, your workplace, your church, and your community?

Chapter Three

YOUR SPHERE OF INFLUENCE

When you hear a message like this one calling you to rise, it may result in you feeling inspired and challenged, or overwhelmed and intimidated. Perhaps even right now you are wondering who, where, and how you can influence.

I have found that in most cases we are already connected to the people and involved in the places and positions where God wants us to be influential. Sometimes, though, we haven't taken the time to notice the impact we have on those around us. Or we haven't seen or taken hold of the opportunities before us because we have lacked the confidence or even the willingness to see ourselves as instruments of influence.

It's important, then, to take a moment to accept two truths:

- You are a woman of influence.
- You can choose to expand your level of influence.

THE BOUNDARIES OF OUR INFLUENCE

We have the ability to impact anyone, anything, and anywhere!

We can influence:

ourselves
individuals
groups
the masses
laws and policies
cultural beliefs
customs and traditions

events
institutions
businesses
churches
governments
communities
environment
cities
nations
rulers of the land
history

The extent of our influence can be so broad and so vast. However, to live life most effectively and fruitfully we need to know specifically who, where, and how we are called to make a difference. That is, we need to be able to define our sphere of influence.

A light always has a distinct area from where it removes the dark and brings brightness. For example, the light from a spotlight is bright, clear, and defined. You can actually see the boundaries of the circle of light. I am convinced of the necessity for each person to "spotlight" the area of their influence.

I am reminded of two pictures I was shown in the journal of one of my coaching clients. The first picture represented how she felt at that present time. The second picture captured her vision for the future and what she wanted to achieve from our coaching sessions together. The first photo was a beautiful old street light, one that you might see in the streets of London. It was made of iron and was tall and ornate. It was bringing light to the street, but its light was dim and diffused.

The second picture was a laser light, its beam narrow, strong, and sharp. The light was powerful because it was focused and defined. My client had labeled this picture "Secret weapon." She had recognized that she was already an instrument of influence, represented by the street light. However, her desire was to increase her level of influence by clarifying her specific sphere of influence. That is by defining who, where, and how she was to make a difference. In this way her life would be more efficient and effective.

It is my belief that as you clearly define your sphere of influence, you will become more like a laser light and a lethal weapon in the hand of God. Your influence will be more powerful because you will be focusing your time, prayer, and energy into the people, places, and positions to which you have been specifically appointed by God.

PEOPLE, PLACES, AND POSITIONS

I believe every Christian man and woman was created to do a job and have an area of influence, and for that purpose God has positioned each of us with specific people, in certain places, and with distinct positions.

Let me write this in a different way. You will have influence:

- With specific people (who you influence)
- In certain places (where you influence)
- In distinct positions (how you influence)

Let's apply this concept to the Proverbs 31 woman. If you read this passage afresh you will notice that she was a woman who was influential with the people she met, in the places she visited, and in the positions she filled in her everyday life.

- **Who:** The people she impacted were her husband, children, servants, the poor, merchants, businesspeople, farmers, and other citizens throughout her town.
- **Where:** The places she had influence over were her family, her household, the marketplace, the business arena, the rural world, and the wider community.
- **How:** The positions of influence she held included being a wife, mother, household manager, business woman, charitable worker, and community elder.

I believe that Christians are to be an influence both in the church and in the community at large. Therefore you and I will have certain people, places, and positions both in the church and in the community that God has called us to impact. He has strategically placed each one of us in a sphere of influence.

PURPOSE AND PASSION

You will be led to the people, places, and positions in your sphere of influence because of the way you were uniquely created. God planned you for a purpose. He designed you with distinctive passions, personality, and talents to fulfill that purpose. Within your sphere of influence your purpose will unfold.

As a life coach, one of my greatest delights is helping people define their passions and purpose. When a person identifies and works in their area of passion, they thrive. Passion is what brings motivation, joy, contentment, satisfaction, and ambition. It is the fuel that keeps hearts alive and feet in motion.

Passion is the expression of your heart. It's what you love. It's what inspires you. It's what gives you a buzz. Let me ask you:

- **Who do you love to be with?** They are the people you will influence.
- **Where do you love to go?** Those are the places you will influence.
- **What do you love doing?** These are your positions of influence.

Using the Proverbs 31 woman again as an example, let's ask the question, What does she love? First and foremost she loves God. She reverently fears Him and serves Him in her daily life. She loves bringing blessing to her husband and her children. She loves her home and diligently watches over the affairs of her household. She delights in spinning, sewing, and selling the clothes that she makes. She loves business and investing. She enjoys negotiating with merchants and choosing fields to buy. She thrives on working hard and being entrepreneurial. She loves giving to the poor and serving the community.

The director of the women's ministry in our church, Pastor Bernadette Kelsey, was given a mandate from God to raise an army of women. She felt overwhelmed and asked God, "How do I do this?" He replied, "Ask the women what is in their hearts, because that's what they need to be doing." How simple! It starts with our hearts. Inside the heart of every woman lies passion and purpose. Discover and unlock your passions, and these will lead you to the people, the places, and the positions where you can make a difference.

EXAMPLES OF DIFFERENT SPHERES OF INFLUENCE

As I said earlier, it is my conviction that God has for each Christian a role and a purpose to fulfill within the church and in the community. Let's look at some examples.

	Passion Purpose	People	Place	Position
1	Seeing youth find Jesus	Teenagers	Outreach program at a local high school	Team leader
2	Discipling young girls to grow in God	Teenage girls	Small group of 15-year-old girls that meets weekly at a home	Assistant leader
3	Being a "dad" to kids	Boys and girls, ages 6–10	Kids' church	Team helper
4	Leading others in worship	Church congregation and worship team	Sunday meetings	Keyboard player in the worship team
5	Raising money to build church facilities	Church congregation and building funds team	Sunday meetings and special events	Member of building funds team
6	Teaching the Word of God to men	Men, ages 30–50	Men's monthly breakfast	Speaker
7	Helping in practical ways and working with food	Church congregation	Kitchen at church serving morning tea	Team helper
8	Bringing joy and Jesus to old people	Elderly men and women who live in local nursing homes	Outreach program at a local nursing home	Team leader
9	Praying for vision and the needs of church	Members of a prayer group and the people you are praying for	Prayer group	Group member
10	Praying for the sick and seeing the miraculous	Sick people and a member of the healing team	• Healing service • Visiting sick people in their homes or hospitals	Team member

Your unique passions and purpose will also find a place in the community, where there is a vast array of opportunities. Your community includes your circle of family, friends, and neighbors; your place of work or study; local businesses or cafes; and the clubs or organizations where you pursue your interests. Here are some examples:

	Passion Purpose	People	Place	Position
1	Surfing	Surfing buddies	Local beaches and coffee shops	Friend
2	Playing basketball	Basketball team	Basketball events	Friend and Team Member
3	To help at my children's school	Children, other moms, and the teacher	Weekly help reading to children in class	Classroom helper
4	Fighting to save rainforest in local community	Citizens and council staff	Local community and council	Team leader in a action group
5	Helping sick people	Sick patients	Local hospital	Nurse
6	Financial Planning	Clients and work associates	One's own business and people's homes or their small businesses	Business owner
7	Seeing neighbors come to Jesus	Neighbors	Where I live and the homes around me	Neighbor and friend
8	To uphold family values	Families	Government office	State politician
9	To teach science to teenagers	Teenagers, parents, and school staff	Local High School	Science teacher
10	Publishing books	Authors, editors, printers, staff	Publishing company	Publisher

My Story

I would like to share with you how this concept of knowing one's sphere of influence applies in my own life. As a life coach I have spent time defining the different areas of my life.

- My passions are to equip, empower, and inspire people. I love to do this through teaching, preaching, writing, praying, prophesying, coaching, and mentoring.
- My purpose is to unlock the hearts, minds, and lives of people so they can fulfill their God-given potential and call.

The people I influence, the positions I hold, and the places where I serve are a reflection of my passions and purpose.

As a pastor in my church, I oversee a network of people and have a core group of female leaders that I disciple. As a teacher, I lecture in our Bible school on subjects that correspond to my interests—for example, ministry gifts, Proverbs for wise living, money and wealth, and discovering yourself. On occasions I speak at other churches and conferences, where I minister through preaching, praying, and prophesying. In these varied ways I disciple believers and help build my church.

My gifts, passions, and purpose also have an expression in the wider community. I have taught and spoken in a variety of settings, such as school groups, business meetings, community organizations, and adult evening colleges. In my life coaching business I use my pastoring, teaching, and prophetic gifts to impact the lives of people from all walks of life. Many of my clients do not attend church, and their beliefs and lifestyles are not like mine. However, it is in this way that God uses me to be a light to their lives.

EXPANDING INFLUENCE

Enlarge the place of your tent, stretch your tent curtains wide, do not hold back; lengthen your cords, strengthen your stakes. For you will spread out to the right and to the left; your descendants will dispossess nations and settle in their desolate cities.

—ISAIAH 54:2–3

Over the last few years, God has taken my family through an interesting journey that has expanded our sphere of influence. Starting my business has been one area of enlargement.

My family's influence has also expanded in a totally different area. I want to share this story with you, as it may prove a useful example for the inevitable day you, too, will be challenged by God to expand your sphere of influence.

For many years we have lived in the same house in a leafy suburb of Sydney, Australia, and for most of the time our family has had only a handful of relational connections with the people in the neighborhood. For a number of reasons we were neither willing nor easily able to reach out to them.

Geographically, our house is situated at the end of a long driveway. It is very private, so we have little direct contact with our neighbors. Secondly, we chose to send our children to a private Christian school located outside our local community. As a consequence, most of my children's friends, sporting groups, and other interests were located beyond our suburb. Thirdly, our time, energy, and lives were very much focused on church, and nearly all our friends were Christians.

Our world had become small and insular. In reality we had erected invisible walls that geographically and socially separated us from the people living nearby. Our family had little to no influence in our local community. One day, God decided to change our isolation and our indifference. It was a few years ago, about a week before Christmas, when my husband felt a very strong prompting from God that we should move our children from the school they were attending and send them to the local public school. When Pat told me this news it felt like a bomb had gone off in my world. Nothing in me wanted to follow this prompting from God. I knew that our children would find the prospect of moving schools very challenging. For myself, I would miss seeing the other moms at our Christian school, many of whom were my friends.

Up until then God had only spoken to my husband. I had heard nothing, and I was feeling very stressed by this impending decision. I cried out to God that if He was doing this new, radical thing in our life, then I wanted to hear from Him myself. God heard my plea.

Very early one morning I woke with a strong sense that God wanted me to get up and go to the local school. I donned my tracksuit and running shoes and set off. As I walked I felt God was saying to me, "I am sending you to a new land. Just like I called Abraham to a new land, so I am calling you."

I arrived at the school to find that the gates were locked up for the Christmas holidays. I found a way to climb over the high fence and began to walk through the school grounds. At the basketball court I stopped, sat down, and wept. I cried about the challenges and the changes that this move would bring to our lives. I grieved for my kids, and I grieved for myself.

While I was crying I was reminded of something God asked me many years ago when our family returned from living as missionaries in the Philippines. He had posed this question to me, "Amanda, will you go again for me?" I remember at the time finding it difficult to say yes because those two years in the Philippines were so difficult.

On the basketball court in the early hours of that morning, He said to me, "Amanda, this is your 'go.' Will you go again?" In the midst of my tears, I responded with a laugh. "It's only two streets away, God." Then I made my reply and added a request to God. I said, "Yes. But I'll only go if people get saved."

I left those school grounds that day with a fresh sense of mission and purpose. I had a new "land" to take. As I walked home God gave me a scripture to hold on to as a promise that He would look after me and my children: "Do not be afraid, Abram [Amanda, Jacinta, and Tyler]. I am your shield, your very great reward" (Gen. 15:1). I returned from that walk a different woman.

But reality hit home when we announced to our daughter (ten years old) and son (seven years old) that at the end of the holidays they would not be returning to their school. Their response was violent. They both screamed and ran to their rooms, slamming the doors behind them. I vividly remember the range of emotions I felt that day. I was saddened by my children's reactions; however, I had a strong sense of peace that God would look after them. Was it easy? No. My children were in shock for a week. They were angry at us and felt disempowered because they were not involved in the decision-making process. Throughout that first year I heard them say on many occasions that their old school was better, and both of them experienced a sense of loss.

One whole year later, my son, at times, still grieved. This saddened and frustrated me because I did not know how to help him. I prayed, "God, I don't know what to do. You have to change and heal his heart." Shortly afterwards, my son, Tyler, was listening to some music that ironically had been produced by his old school. The message of the song concerned a revolution involving children who would choose to reach out and shine for Jesus in their community. In an instant God gave my son a revelation that changed his life forever. He could now see God's purpose and plan for his own life. He realized his personal call to his new school and the influence that he could have. In excitement he told me, "Mum, I understand now why I am at this school."

From that moment my son began to love his new school, and he has played an instrumental role in leading one of his teachers to Jesus. Both of my children have brought lots of their friends to our church's youth group, and many of them have become Christians. I love the fact that God doesn't just call and commission moms and dads. Our children also have a sphere of influence where they can make a positive difference in other people's lives. Since moving schools our sphere of influence has also broadened into other areas, such as the interest groups and sporting clubs my children have joined.

The Bible says that "the increase of His government and peace there will be no end" (Isa. 9:7). To me this means that the kingdom of God will always be growing and enlarging. As Christians, our sphere of influence can and possibly should be continually increasing. In a number of parables, Jesus promises, "When you have been faithful with the little then I will give you more" (Matt. 25:23, author's paraphrase).

Jesus will give you more of whatever He gave you to begin with. It could be talents, spiritual gifts, money, people, responsibilities, or influence. We need to be diligent and faithful with whomever and whatever God has given to us. Then we must be prepared for our reward for the job well done: to be given more. I have given this principle a title, The Law of Ever-Increasing Influence. We actually joke about it in our house because we have seen it operate time and time again. When you do a job diligently and with excellence, God gives you a bigger job. Do well with the bigger job, then you get an even bigger job. Do well with the even bigger job... And so it goes on. I can assure you this biblical principle will also operate in your life, because our God is in the business of increase.

THE STORY OF ESTHER, A WOMAN OF INFLUENCE

The Book of Esther in the Old Testament tells the inspiring story of Esther, a remarkable woman who used her influence to bring about the deliverance of the nation and people of Israel. She was a humble young woman who was appointed by God to connect with specific people in certain places. She was to hold a distinguished position, as God had a task for her to perform so as to fulfill His purpose.

Esther, a Jewish orphan, was brought up in the house of her kind and loving uncle, Mordecai. They lived at a time when the nation of Israel was governed by the Persians. There was turmoil, however, in the royal courts, because the queen of Persia, Vashti, had brought dishonor to her husband, King Xerxes. The king responded by seeking to replace Vashti with a new wife and a new queen.

Esther, along with many other beautiful virgins, was chosen to live in the king's harem. All the virgins were groomed and prepared to become the next queen of Persia, but only one of them would capture the eyes and the heart of the king. The one that shone above all the others was Esther. She was raised up and crowned the queen of Persia. But the king was unaware that he was marrying a Jewish girl.

Meanwhile, an evil man by the name of Haman was working in the palace courts with Esther's uncle, Mordecai. Haman despised Mordecai because Mordecai did not show the respect due to him as a higher-ranking official. Haman therefore plotted Mordecai's demise. The Bible says, "When Haman saw that Mordecai would not kneel down or pay him honor, he was enraged. Yet having learned who Mordecai's people were, he scorned the idea of killing only Mordecai. Instead Haman looked for a way to destroy all Mordecai's people, the Jews, throughout the whole kingdom of Xerxes" (Esther 3:5–6). So, Haman wrote a decree to exterminate the entire Israelite people, cunningly persuading the king to sign and seal the edict with his signet ring.

Mordecai heard of the decree detailing his people's impending death. Immediately he called upon his niece, Esther, and besought her to go to the king and beg for mercy on behalf of all the Jewish people. He said these challenging words:

Do not think that because you are in the king's house you alone of all the Jews will escape. For if you remain silent at this time, relief and deliverance for the Jews will arise from another place, but you and your father's family will perish. And who knows but that you have come to royal position for such a time as this?

—ESTHER 4:12–14

Esther knew the cost of approaching the king without being summoned. Xerxes had the power to deny anyone entry into his presence. The law even stated that any person who approached the king could be put to death. That person could only be spared if the king extended his gold scepter. Esther was fearful of the law and her husband. But the words of her uncle saturated her soul. Esther knew that she had been placed in this position and in this place to bring about the purposes of God: the deliverance of the Jewish race from genocide. She sought help from her people. For three days they fasted and prayed that Esther would have favor as she approached the king.

A courageous Esther entered the king's presence, and the gold scepter was extended. She had gained the first favor. Esther invited the king and Haman to attend a banquet that she had prepared for them. The king approved, and both he and Haman attended the banquet, at which time Esther invited them both to return the next day for another feast. They both accepted her invitation. The second and third favors had been won.

At the banquet the king asked, "Queen Esther, what is your petition?" (Esther 7:2). She told him of the edict to annihilate the Jews and that it had been devised by the other guest dining at the table, the vile Haman. Xerxes was furious and ordered Haman's immediate death. Ironically, Haman's execution took place on the very same gallows that he had erected to execute Mordecai. The enemy was now defeated; Esther had found favor a fourth time.

The edict to destroy the Jews was revoked by Xerxes. Not only were the Jewish people saved that day, but they were empowered to rise and destroy their enemies. Thousands of people who hated the Jews were put to death. Favor was granted yet again. On that significant day the Jewish people were delivered, and their dignity and joy returned. Queen Esther had one final request of the king: for Haman's sons to be hanged. For the sixth time favor was bestowed upon her, and the ten sons were executed.

Interestingly, what happened to Esther's uncle is a great example of the Law of Ever-Increasing Influence! We meet him at the beginning of the book as a royal official sitting at the king's gate (Esther 2:19; 3:2), and even though the evil Haman tried to have him executed, God arranged for him to be noticed and favored by the king. In the middle of the story we see Mordecai honored by the king for uncovering the conspiracy to have the king assassinated (Esther 2, 6).

After the edict to kill the Jews was revoked, Mordecai was promoted. No longer was he sitting outside at the gates. Now he was given a position of honor and authority inside the palace. He was draped in royal garments, and a crown was placed upon his head. The Bible says, "Mordecai was prominent in the palace; his reputation spread throughout the provinces, and he became more and more powerful" (Esther 9:4). The book concludes, "Mordecai the Jew was second in rank to King Xerxes, preeminent among the Jews, and held in high esteem by his many fellow Jews, because he worked for the good of his people and spoke up for the welfare of all the Jews" (Esther 10:3). It is clear that both Esther and Mordecai were raised up by God to be significant players in that moment in Jewish history.

The star of the story, Esther, had a well-defined sphere of influence. Her place was the Persian palace, and her position was that of queen. The king of Persia and the Jewish people were the people she was called to influence. We can see in the life of Esther that when we live and operate in our sphere of influence we will find the favor of God at work in our lives. He will open doors of opportunity, provide divine connections, and bring blessings beyond the limits of our imagination. We will see our own calling being realized but also—most importantly—the fulfillment of the purposes of God. What does it take? It takes us being willing to rise at such a time to such a position for such a purpose!

THE PROVERBS 31 WOMAN

A wife of noble character who can find? She is worth far more than rubies. Her husband has full confidence in her and lacks nothing of value. She brings him good, not harm, all the days of her life. She selects wool and flax works with eager hands. She is like the merchant ships, bringing her food from afar. She gets up while it is still dark; she provides food for her family and portions for her servant girls. She considers a field and buys it; out of her earnings she plants a vineyard. She sets about her work vigorously; her arms are strong for her tasks. She sees that her trading is profitable, and her lamp does not go out at night. In her hand she holds the distaff and grasps the spindle with her fingers. She opens her arms to the poor and extends her hands to the needy. When it snows, she has no fear for her household; for all of them are clothed in scarlet. She makes coverings for her bed; she is clothed in fine linen and purple. Her husband is respected at the city gate, where he takes his seat among the elders of the land. She makes linen garments and sells them, and supplies the merchants with sashes. She is clothed with strength and dignity; she can laugh at the days to come. She speaks with wisdom, and faithful instruction is on her tongue. She watches over the affairs of her household and does not eat the bread of idleness. Her children arise and call her blessed; her husband also, and he praises her: "Many women do noble things, but you surpass them all." Charm is deceptive, and beauty is fleeting; but a woman who fears the LORD is to be praised. Give her the reward she has earned, and let her works bring her praise at the city gate.

—PROVERBS 31:10–31

TIME TO REFLECT

God has created you with distinct passions and purpose. These will lead you to certain people, places, and positions both in the church and in the community where you can be an influence.

Take a moment to identify the answers to the following questions. Respond in the context of both your influence in the community and in the church you attend.

- What am I passionate about? Who, what, and where does my heart love?
- How do I want to contribute or make a difference in this world?
- Who are the people in my world that I can and do influence?
- Where are the places I can and do have influence?
- What positions do I hold where I can and do have influence?
- Is God expanding your sphere of influence? If so, in what way?
- Finish, this statement: "My sphere of influence is…"

TIME TO ACT

- Does your work in the community and your area of service in the church correspond to your passions and purpose? If not, what can you do about it? Brainstorm ideas about different areas of responsibility or work that would better express your purpose and passions. Identify what it would mean for you to pursue the best idea or ideas.

Chapter Four

WHY MUST WE RISE?

God has dreams.

He can see the future.

He sees heaven filled with people
  from every nation, tribe, and people group
    worshiping the glorious, risen Jesus
      forever and ever and ever and ever.

He can see the present.
  He has dreams for today and for tomorrow.
    He dreams of His glory covering all the Earth.
      He dreams of every person embracing Jesus.
        He dreams of nations proclaiming His name.

But God sees war.
  He sees the kingdom of light
    battling with the kingdom of darkness.
      He sees evil. He sees pain.
        He sees deception. He sees rebellion.

Yet God has a plan.

He will use His people.
  He will use the church
    to bring light into dark places,
      to bring truth, to bring hope,
        to bring freedom, to bring salvation.

Yes, God has dreams, and we are a part of them.

Why must we rise?

To answer this question, we need to be reminded of God's dreams and the part we play in fulfilling them. We need to be reminded that it is the church and the people of God that carry His presence, glory, and light into dark lives and dark places. It is Christians filled with the love and power of God who can bring the gospel to every person living in every home, street, suburb, town, city, state, and nation across the globe.

> *From the days of John the Baptist until now, the kingdom of heaven has been forcefully advancing, and forceful men lay hold of it.*
> —MATTHEW 11:12

I get so stirred by this scripture. When God first enlightened this verse to me, my spirit roared. These words spoken by Jesus are not gentle words. He declares that God's kingdom is mighty; it is ever-increasing and always advancing. And it is doing this forcefully, which means vigorously and violently. The kingdom of light is convincingly and dynamically breaking through the opposing kingdom of darkness. We might be at war, but there's good news: we are on the winning side.

In going about our daily lives we can so easily forget or be oblivious to the fact that we are in the midst of a raging supernatural battle. Every now and then we need to be reminded that we are involved in this war and that God has called us to be soldiers in His army. As the scripture says, we are to be forceful—strong, aggressive, powerful, vigorous, and influential men and women. That's what we are called to be. That's what we are called to do.

The kingdom of God is only forcefully advancing because forceful men and women are laying hold of it. I believe God is yearning for forceful Christians who will fight battles and take ground for the expansion of the kingdom of light, men and women who will lay their lives down for the King of kings and His cause. This is the mission that beats in the heart of God and why He is calling His women to arise, shine, and be people of influence.

I am fully persuaded that God's plans and purposes are locked up and His kingdom weakened when Christians don't rise to the fullness of their potential and calling. Therefore, we need to be women filled with the fire of vision who will push through fear and rise to be people of influence within the land that God has placed us. Only then will God's kingdom come on Earth.

PROPHETIC MANDATE

When I had the encounter with God on my bed, which I have described in the Introduction, the first words I wrote in my notebook were:

Write a prophetic mandate to my women.
Tell them it is their time to rise; it is their time to shine.

To be quite honest I was initially taken aback by the words *prophetic mandate*. It seemed a big expression, and it took me a while to understand its significance.

Let me begin by unraveling the meaning of these two important words:

- *Prophetic* refers to receiving a message from God as a word or vision that is relevant for now or for the future.
- *Mandate* is an order, a command, or a directive given by someone in authority.

When God said the words, "It is their time to *rise*, it is their time to *shine*," I believe that He was giving us both a message and a command. He was speaking directly from heaven and telling us an instruction to follow. In my heart I know that this prophecy and this mandate is for women, and it is for now.

To fully appreciate and embrace this directive, it is important to understand this prophetic word in the larger and broader context of what God is saying and doing in churches and in His kingdom throughout the world. This will also help us to answer the question, Why must we rise?

God speaks appointed words at appointed times for appointed purposes! He never changes, but the seasons and the times change. That is why God speaks through His prophets, who reveal, through the Holy Spirit, what God is doing in the new season and in the new time. It is imperative, then, that we know and understand the prophetic words God is speaking about *now*, about the *new*, and about the *future*.

Surely the Sovereign LORD *does nothing without revealing his plan to his servants the prophets.*

—AMOS 3:7

In this chapter I am going to quote prophetic words that have been spoken in this new century by various people in various places. Many of these words have been proclaimed by my pastor, Phil Pringle, to the congregation of C3 Church, Sydney, Australia. Based on the prophecies declared in my church and on the preaching of other ministers across the globe, I know that God is speaking a fresh word and doing a new thing in the twenty-first century. It is not just in my church or in my city or in my nation, but across the face of the entire earth.

There are four main prophetic themes that have been declared in the early part of this new century that are still in the process of being fulfilled today. These themes are:

1. The river
2. The walls are coming down
3. Seven pillars of influence
4. God is raising an army

Prophetic words often come in images or metaphors, so it is necessary to interpret their meaning and how they may be applied to the church and to our own lives. What follows is my prayerful interpretation of these four prophetic themes. It is important to recognize that prophecy should not be regarded as something that must happen. Rather, prophecy speaks of possibility. Prophetic words often have conditions that must be acted upon in order for the word to be fulfilled. We must take heed to them through prayer and action.

THE PROPHETIC THEMES OF
THE TWENTY-FIRST CENTURY

1. The River

Whoever believes in me, as the Scripture has said, streams of living water will flow from within him.

—JOHN 7:38

In the mid 1990s God brought revival to His church. It was named "the river" by many. The river brought laughter, healing, freedom, and some bizarre manifestations; but most significantly it brought fire and fresh life into the hearts of Christians.

Since the early 2000s, many of the prophetic words spoken have again referred to the river, this time however with a different emphasis. In the twentieth century, the river was an encounter with God that generally took place in the church environment. It brought personal revival. In the twenty-first century the river seems no longer to be just an experience that is to be contained within the church. Rather, Christians are to be filled with this river, then take and transfer its life and power to people in the world. It is this river that will bring salvation, healing, and deliverance. Here are excerpts from two different prophecies that speak about the river.

As I am standing here I can feel a river pouring all around my legs. It is a river of life. In this river of life the fish swim, people get saved, and in this river there is healing wherever it travels. This river of life will come out of your belly as you speak the word of God.

—PHIL PRINGLE
JULY 13, 2003

I will come to you like a river of fresh water—fresh, healing water—and out of your belly will flow this river of living water. As you involve your-self with other people in fellowship and as you reach out to other people who have not met me, I will flow out of you like a river, out of your belly, rivers of living water. And understand this, the works that I did, you will do also. The very same works of healing I did, you will do also; the very same works of deliverance I did, you will do also.

You will lay hands on the blind, and their eyes will be opened. Some of you will lay hands on the deaf, and their ears will be unstopped. Some of you will lay your hands on the crippled, and they will walk. Some of you will lay your hands on those who are sick and diseased in their flesh, and they will be healed. You will do the same works that Jesus did on the face of the earth, but not only will you do the same but you will do greater works than those...

Understand I do not give you the Holy Spirit for your own emotional well-being only. I give you the Holy Spirit so you can minister Him to other people and minister Him to those who have not yet met Jesus. As you minister the power of the Holy Spirit, as you release this power that I have given you, as you freely give what you have been freely given, you will find the sick will be healed, you will find their circumstances will find solutions. You will speak my word and you will be strong. You will not be weak as my representatives. You will be strong. You will not just be the people of God, you will be the sons of the Most High.

You will walk as sons and daughters with authority that I give you, as I clothe you with my authority, as I clothe you with my power. So my Spirit will fall upon you, so my presence will come upon you, so my power will come upon you, so my river will flow through you.'

—Phil Pringle
September 28, 2003

These prophetic words powerfully correspond to a vision seen by the prophet Ezekiel a few thousand years ago.

The man brought me back to the entrance of the temple, and I saw water coming out from under the threshold of the temple toward the east (for the temple faced east). The water was coming down from under the south side of the temple, south of the altar. He then brought me out through the north gate and led me around the outside to the outer gate facing east, and the water was flowing from the south side.

As the man went eastward with a measuring line in his hand, he measured off a thousand cubits and then led me through water that was ankle-deep. He measured off another thousand cubits and led me through water that was knee-deep. He measured off another thousand and led me through water that was up to the waist. He measured off another thousand, but now it was a river that I could not cross, because the water had risen and was deep enough to swim in—a river that no one could cross. He asked me, "Son of man, do you see this?" Then he led me back to the bank of the river. When I arrived there, I saw a great number of trees on each side of the river. He said to me, "This water flows toward the eastern region and goes down into the Arabah, where it enters the Sea. When it empties into the Sea, the water there becomes fresh. Swarms of living creatures will live wherever the river flows. There will be large numbers of fish, because this water flows there and makes the salt water fresh; so where the river flows everything will live. Fishermen will stand along the shore; from En Gedi to En Eglaim there will be places for spreading nets. The fish will be of many kinds—like the fish of the Great Sea. But the swamps and marshes will not become fresh; they will be left for salt. Fruit trees of all kinds will grow on both banks of the river. Their leaves will not wither, nor will their fruit fail. Every month they will bear, because the water from the sanctuary flows to them. Their fruit will serve for food and their leaves for healing.

—EZEKIEL 47:1–12

Ezekiel's vision describes a beautiful freshwater river coming out from under a temple. The farther the river flows from the temple, the wider and deeper it becomes. It grows so large and so powerful that no one can cross it. Eventually it meets the potent, salty water of the Dead Sea. At this junction the water becomes fresh, and there is a profusion of fish, which are being caught in the nets of the fishermen. Along the banks are lush fruit trees, which are growing in abundance. Wherever the river runs there is prolific, glorious life.

To understand the significance of this vision and its relevance to the prophecies that are being spoken today, we need to ask a few questions: What is the temple? What is the river? What is the Dead Sea? What are the fish? And when and to whom does this prophecy apply?

First and foremost, I believe this prophecy is relevant to the here and now and to you and me. This vision reflects God's plan for believers, the church, and the Earth today. The temple is the church, and the river is the presence of God, which is the Holy Spirit dwelling within every Christian. The Dead Sea is reflective of people, cities, and nations that are living in darkness. In this vision, transformation occurs when the freshwater river meets the salty, lifeless sea. This symbolizes what happens today when Christians take the love and power of God to a lost and dying world. The fish are those people whose lives will be radically changed as they encounter the presence and power of God.

This prophecy is a call for Christians to go out from our church meetings, purposefully carrying the presence and power of the Spirit into every area of our lives. We can take the truth, freedom, healing, and salvation we have received from Jesus to the people that we meet. When we do this the river is flowing. This prophecy reminds us that God does not intend His presence and power to be confined to church meetings and to the minister in the pulpit. Rather, His Spirit is alive and at work in each and every one of us, wherever we are. It's interesting to note that the river becomes deeper and more powerful the farther away it travels from the temple. What a revolutionary thought! God's presence is supposed to be stronger out in the world than in the church building or in church meetings.

These prophecies, spoken around 570 B.C. and in the year A.D. 2003, are calling us to be bold believers who will minister healing and salvation to those who do not yet know Jesus. We can be this river in our workplaces, at the shops, in our families, at our schools, in our sporting clubs—anywhere and everywhere God has placed us. Jesus has called us to be "fishers of men" (Mark 1:17). In this simple way we have the potential to gather many "fish" and advance the kingdom of God.

Out of you, out of you will flow rivers, rivers of life—rivers that will make the dead to rise, rivers that will heal the sick, rivers that will bring joy where there is depression, rivers that will bring hope to the despairing, rivers that will bring new days to those that have died.

—PHIL PRINGLE
NOVEMBER 23, 2003

2. The Walls Are Coming Down

For he himself is our peace, who has made the two one and has destroyed the barrier, the dividing wall of hostility.

—EPHESIANS 2:14

As I stepped out of bed one morning, my spirit heard these words being loudly proclaimed from heaven: "The walls are coming down!" I also saw an image of a walled city, one like the city of Jericho, and its walls were slowly crumbling to the ground, brick by brick by brick. A number of months later I was attending a conference at our church. During a powerful time of worship, the congregation prophetically sang a refrain that we repeated over and over; it reflected this same vision of walls coming down and chains breaking.

For some time these words mystified me. I kept asking God, "What do they mean? What and where are these walls? How are they coming down, and what does this signify?" I sought to understand this prophetic proclamation by searching the Scriptures and seeking God. Let me share with you what I discovered.

In Bible times, walls were built as a means of protection and fortification because of the hostility between two opposing peoples, nations, or kingdoms. The walls provided a physical barrier that kept the two worlds separate and safe from each other. When a walled city had its gates closed, no one could either enter or leave. The people inside were shut in, and the people outside were shut out. The walls both divided and contained the people.

I believe the interpretation of this prophecy is that there are thick, impenetrable walls dividing and separating the people in the church and people in the world. This has resulted in feelings of hostility between the two different "camps" and an "us and them" mentality. Some Christians have erected these walls by choosing to live apart or detached from the people and the communities surrounding them. The bricks that make up these walls come from a multitude of different sources. They include indifference, distraction, confusion, judgment, and fear. Each of these factors will be explored in more detail but it is important to say up front that these walls are one of Satan's schemes. They have resulted in isolation and exclusion.

When they are pulled down, the devil is defeated and the kingdom of God is advanced.

It is common to find that the lives of many Christians revolve predominantly around the church and its people. Often much of their time and energy is directed toward serving in the church and socializing with believers. This involvement is important, but if it leaves no room for mixing with people outside the church, then it becomes a problem. When we do this we have built a dividing wall, effectively isolating and excluding ourselves from those who are lost and needing Jesus. In the previous chapter, I shared how our family had done this and what God led us to do to bring down the wall we had erected. For us, the problem was indifference. We had become complacent to the need and our responsibility to reach the lost.

I believe these walls have also been built because there is confusion in some Christians' minds about what it means to be holy.

The concept of holiness has evolved throughout the Bible. In the Old Testament, God called His people, the Israelites, to be a holy people and a holy nation. He chose to physically separate the Israelites from the other nations by giving them the Promised Land. This land, and its walled capital city, Jerusalem, were set apart for the Israelites to live in. God also required them to live pure lives by following laws that stipulated such things as how they worshiped, what they ate, how they cooked, what they wore, and who they married. Under the old covenant, God instituted holiness by geographically separating His people and demanding obedience to the Law.

For us today, living under the new covenant still demands that we live pure lives. But we do this now by following the leading of the Holy Spirit, not by obeying the requirements of the Law. Another radical difference is that we are no longer required to geographically live separately from others. Our promised land is now not a physical place but rather the abundance of good things that we inherit from God, which we are then supposed to pass on to others.

It has been my observation that some believers have chosen to place themselves in what I would call a cocoon because they fear that the world will taint or harm them in some way. As holy Christians we must remain consecrated and set apart to live for Him, but this does not mean we disconnect ourselves from those we are called to reach. It is important that we find the balance of being in the world but not of the world. The apostle Peter provides us with insight into this.

> *But you are a chosen people, a royal priesthood, a holy nation, a people belonging to God, that you may declare the praises of him who called you out of darkness into his wonderful light. Once you were not a people, but now you are the people of God; once you had not received mercy, but now you have received mercy. Dear friends, I urge you, as aliens and strangers in the world, to abstain from sinful desires, which war against your soul. Live such good lives among the pagans that, though they accuse you of doing wrong, they may see your good deeds and glorify God on the day he visits us.*
>
> —1 PETER 2:9–12

God's Word here tells us about our past and our present. It says that we were once living in darkness with no experience of mercy, and we were distant from God. But now things are different. Now we live in His wonderful light. And we now belong to Him because we have received His beautiful mercy. Now it is our job to help others experience this transition and transformation.

This scripture gives us a title. We are called a royal priesthood! What does it mean to be a priest? In the Old Testament the priest was a mediator who performed the sacrifices for the people's sins and talked to God on their behalf. In simple terms the priest was the go-between, the one who connected God to the people and the people to God.

Such is our role today. We are the ones called to be bridges between those who do not know God and God Himself. Sometimes these people aren't yet ready or willing to see God, so they need us: a go-between, someone who reflects God but also leads them to Him. Through our lives they can see His mercy, love, light, and transforming grace and power. What a difference for us to be bridges that connect rather than walls that divide!

I believe a further reason why some Christians have put up dividing walls and retreated from connecting with others is the fact that we are aliens and strangers in the world. If you are a holy Christian, then you will be different to the people in the world, so different, in fact, that you will feel at times like a stranger, a foreigner, or an alien—like someone from another planet.

Well, I want to declare loud and clear, that's exactly what you are! You are from another kingdom! No longer are you in the kingdom of darkness; you are now a citizen of the kingdom of heaven. Everything about you is different: your beliefs, your values, and your behaviors. Because of this difference, some Christians have become judgmental or fearful. Others have felt uncomfortable and retreated from connecting with non-Christians. It is this difference that will cause some people in the world to be repelled by us, others to be mystified, and still others to be attracted. It is this difference that gives us the authority to influence.

All Christians need to recognize and accept the fact that we are called to be different. But in our difference we cannot put up walls that would divide or separate us from the people and the communities that we are called to impact. God is challenging us afresh to be His ambassador and walk boldly into this foreign kingdom. He needs us to be His representative. Jesus actually prayed for us that we would be empowered and protected while we do this.

> *I have given them your word and the world has hated them, for they are not of the world any more than I am of the world. My prayer is not that you take them out of the world but that you protect them from the evil one. They are not of the world, even as I am not of it. Sanctify them by the truth; your word is truth. As you sent me into the world, I have sent them into the world.*
>
> —JOHN 17:14–18

First Peter 2:9–12 also tells us our strategy. It's so easy and so simple. We are to live good lives and do good deeds. This revolutionary approach could actually bring about revival—a revolution of love and action that will see Christians all around the globe being awakened to more fully live the Christian life by reaching out to their neighbors and strangers through simple acts of kindness. If we will take the time to eat, play, laugh, and talk with those who do not yet know God, hearts will be touched and won to Jesus.

In this way the walls that have divided and separated will come tumbling to the ground, brick by brick by brick...

I love the following scriptures about the city of Jerusalem and how the walls surrounding this city were going to be destroyed. I believe they convey an exciting picture for the church and the community of today. Instead of the dividing walls of the past, there will be invisible walls of salvation, fire, and the presence of God.

> *He will bring down your high fortified walls and lay them low; he will bring them down to the ground, to the very dust.... In that day this song will be sung in the land of Judah: We have a strong city; God makes salvation its walls and ramparts.*
>
> —Isaiah 25:12; 26:1

> *Then I looked up—and there before me was a man with a measuring line in his hand! I asked, "Where are you going?" He answered me, "To measure Jerusalem, to find out how wide and how long it is." Then the angel who was speaking to me left, and another angel came to meet him and said to him: "Run, tell that young man, 'Jerusalem will be a city without walls because of the great number of men and livestock in it. And I myself will be a wall of fire around it,' declares the LORD, 'and I will be its glory within.'"*
>
> —Zechariah 2:1–5

3. Seven Pillars of Influence

There is a prophetic message currently being preached around the world that is calling Christians to rise and be an influence in every pillar or sphere of society. I have personally heard this message spoken by two preeminent ministers: Kong Hee from City Harvest Church in Singapore, and Sunday Adelaja from Embassy of God Church in Kiev, the Ukraine. Both of these men pastor churches of over twenty thousand members.

There are primarily seven pillars in any society. These seven spheres of influence transcend any culture, race, or nation. The preachers and authors around the world who speak and write on this topic use different words to describe these seven pillars, I have chosen the following:

1. Spiritual, social, and health
2. Art, culture, and sport
3. Politics
4. Business
5. Education
6. Mass media
7. Family

These seven pillars represent the areas that shape and influence our society. They encompass the financial, cultural, social, political, spiritual, educational, and recreational spheres, which form the backbone of our societies. It's important, therefore, for Christians to rise to prominent positions in each of these seven pillars. We need men and women who will take the heart and mind of God and be an influence and a voice for Him in these different areas of society. For nations to be impacted for Jesus, it is essential that kingdom values and strategies shape these seven spheres. Pastor Kong Hee's conviction is that our job is not just to convert individuals. Our role is bigger and broader than this. We are to convert society.

Bob Briner argues in an extract from his book Roaring Lambs that Christians have set up their own subculture within society and that because of this we have undermined our effectiveness for being an influence for change in the broader context of society. He says:

Despite all the fancy buildings, sophisticated programs and highly visible presence, it is my contention that the church is almost a nonentity when it comes to shaping culture. In the arts, entertainment, media, education, and other culture shaping venues of our country, the church has abdicated its role as salt and light...Culturally, we are lambs. Meek, lowly, easily dismissed, cuddly creatures that are fun to watch but never a threat to the status quo...We feel we are making a difference because we are so important to ourselves. We have created a phenomenal subculture with our own media, entertainment, educational system and political hierarchy so that we have the sense that we're doing a lot. But what we've really done is created a ghetto that is easily dismissed by the rest of society.[1]

He continues:

> *It's time for the lambs to roar. What I'm calling for is a radically different way of thinking about our world. Instead of running from it, we need to rush into it. And instead of just hanging around the fringes of our culture, we need to be right smack dab in the middle of it...I believe it's not only possible but absolutely necessary for Christians and Christian values to become a vital element in the overall moral and cultural discourse of our nation...If we are obedient to our Lord's call to go into all the world, we will begin reentering the fields we have fled. Are you ready to roar?[2]*

I believe God is doing two significant new things. First, He is raising believers to be His ambassadors in these seven pillars of society. His desire is that Christian men and women will be elite athletes, politicians, directors in influential businesses, leaders of major institutions, stars on the silver screen, and owners of media empires. God needs believers to be the leaders, the decision makers, and the innovators who will shape society now and in the future.

Second, God is enlarging and shifting the way we have seen and done things.

From:
The church gathered
for the meeting on Sunday
to hear the minister and the message,
to experience the presence and power of God,
to build and transform our own lives.

To include:
The church scattered
everywhere we are, every day of the week,
with every believer a Holy-Spirit–empowered minister
taking the presence of God out into the world
and transforming peoples' lives and our societies.

Che Ahn declares, "Now is the time for every believer to come forth into their true identity and confidence as heirs and sons and daughters of God!

That means it is time for ministry in the workplace. It is time for the miraculous to become normal. It is time to take prophecy and other spiritual gifts outside of the four walls of the church. It is time to transform society by obeying the mandate to disciple whole nations. Everywhere I travel I am seeing nobodies arising and doing the works of God with the same power and results as Jesus. They have no thought for themselves or their reputations. They are radical in their prayers, their passion and their pursuit. God is initiating this move and our only job is to let go and yield to it."[3]

How exciting! This is what will happen across the globe when Christians take the power of God they have experienced in their churches out into their communities. This is the river of God in operation! This is how individual lives, societies, cities, and nations will be touched and transformed by the power of God and how His glory will cover all the Earth.

Phil Pringle has prophesied on a number of occasions about how the people in my church will be used by God to be an influence in these different pillars of society that will result in the city in which I live, Sydney, and my nation, Australia, being transformed by the power of God. I believe these prophetic words can be applied to your church, your city and your nation.

> *"I am about to visit the high places of Sydney (Australia). I am about to visit the government of this city. I am about to visit the leadership of this city. I am about to visit the financial leadership of this city. And I will visit them through my people. I will give you open doors," says the Lord, "by the power of my Spirit. I am going to do these things rapidly. The move of my Spirit will accelerate in this city. I will visit those in the entertainment industry, I will visit those in the sporting world, and even now," says the Lord, "I am putting my touch on your life for great things, not for small things. I have ordained you for greatness," says the almighty God. "Lift up your heart, lift up your voice, lift up your spirit to me; and I will touch you by my Spirit. I will do these things," says the almighty God…"I aim to shake this city," says the Lord. "I aim to reach this nation," says the Holy Spirit. "I will do it through you."*
>
> —Phil Pringle
> September 7, 2003

4. God Is Raising an Army

So I prophesied as he commanded me, and breath entered them; they came to life and stood up on their feet—a vast army.

—EZEKIEL 37:10

The fourth theme that is being declared by prophets in recent years is that God is raising an army of men and women.

"For it is a day of increasing darkness on the Earth. The minds of people are becoming increasingly blackened with the darkness of hell. But I will shine brighter in this hour than I have ever shone before," says the Lord. "As darkness increases, so will my glory, and I will shine upon those people whose hearts are truly mine... So be strong, and equip yourselves like great men and women of God. Be strong in the Lord and in the power of His might, for attack after attack will come, but you will be strong and unmovable, unshakeable in the ways of the Most High God. As you are planted in the house of the Lord and planted in the Word of God and planted in the place of prayer, you will become immovable as waves of tribulation come against the church. But even in this hour," says the Lord, "I will raise up an army that is mighty. I will raise up a people who are strong by my Spirit. I will raise up a great army that will spread themselves across the Earth. This will be an army of light, who are clothed with the shield of faith, who are clothed with the armor of light."

—PHIL PRINGLE
AUGUST 3, 2003

"We together will rise up as this exceedingly great and mighty army... I am calling a whole company of women," says the Lord. "I am calling an exceedingly great and glorious army," says the Lord, "who will fill this earth, and who will fill the cities."

—CHRISTINE PRINGLE
C3 WOMEN'S CONFERENCE
OCTOBER 24, 2003

I remember there was a particular day when I sought God to help me understand how I could apply this prophetic word to myself, especially as I live in a peaceful country and have had no experience of war or fighting. I wanted to grasp what this army of women looked like and what it meant to be a female soldier. I asked God to show me a picture, a vision, or an image of this army. On other occasions when I have asked a similar question, God has shown me amazing things. This time was different. I had a strong impression that day that He wasn't going to show me anything. Rather, He wanted me to use my own imagination.

So imagine I did, and I began to write down what I personally envisioned about God's army of women. I have recorded here what I allowed myself to imagine. I entitled my dream of God's army of women "I See…" My prayer is that this picture will inspire you to take your rightful place in His army. As soldiers, each of us must know our position and place and be prepared to courageously fight. We need to put on our combat gear, take up our sword, and march into battle. It is our choice to be forceful women who will violently and vigorously advance the kingdom of God.

I SEE…

I see a multitude of women from different cultures, ages, and social classes signing up to join the army to fight for Jesus, their King. They will be committed to the cause of their King: that His glory will cover all the Earth and His kingdom will be established. These women will play a part in seeing the gospel preached to their friends, families, and work mates, and to every tribe, people group, and nation across the globe. They will be committed to their King's cause, which is to build the church. Women in God's army will be used to bring justice and truth on the Earth and freedom to those who are politically and socially oppressed.

I see women who have placed their life at the feet of Jesus and said, "Here I am; use me." I see God placing His hand on their head, filling them with His power, and saying, "Run!" I see women who have heard and felt the heartbeat of their God. There are women in schools, cafés, offices, mother's groups, shops, kindergartens, gyms, government offices, hospitals, law courts, police stations, television—women in every facet of life shining the life, love, and truth of Jesus. They are being the lights of the world and the salt of the Earth.

Where there are sad hearts, women are listening. Where there are sick bodies, I see faith-filled women praying. Where there are confused minds, women are counseling and giving wisdom. Where there are lonely hearts, there are friends nearby. I see women laughing, crying, touching, praying, hugging, worshiping, and serving. I see women in the business world making decisions, influencing the economy, and making money, which will empower ministries all over the globe. I see women in the political world who will uphold truth and life.

I see women with pure hearts and pure lives. I see women who respect their husbands and who love and care for their children. They are great home-makers and committed servants in the house of God. I see women who are physically and emotionally tough, women who are disciplined with their time and talents and who single-mindedly pursue the call of God for their life. I see strong women who are bold and courageous breaking through their own personal fears. I see women who are free and being transformed from glory to glory. I see women armed with the power of the Word and filled with the Holy Spirit. These women know who they are and whose they are. They are daughters of the Father, princesses of the King, and warriors in the army of God. They are beautiful, liberated, gentle, feminine, strong, capable, disciplined, prepared, equipped, and competent. They are enflamed with vision, passion, and purpose.

I see women walking boldly into the devil's domain and their prayers pushing back darkness. I see women snatching souls from hell and bringing people into the kingdom of light. I see women fighting the good fight and running their race. I see men and women partnering together. They are working in powerful teams, building the church, influencing society, and expanding the kingdom of God.

These four prophetic messages are simple, but their mission is profound. You and I have a decision to make. Will we rise to be women who fulfill these prophecies? Will we embrace their challenge and take up their cause? Will we be the river that carries the power and presence of God into our communities? Will we be bridges that connect, not walls that divide and separate? Will we be soldiers who fight the devil and take back our territory? Will we rise and be women of influence in one of the seven pillars of society?

Why must we rise? Throughout the ages, the answer to this question has remained the same. It's all about the harvest. God's dreams, purposes, and plans are all directed toward people meeting Jesus—the one who created them, died for them, and wants to live with them forever. He chose you and me to be salt and light to this world. He chose us to fulfill His dream. I would like to finish this chapter with one last prophecy that I believe summarizes the heart and purposes of God in the twenty-first century.

"The Spirit of the Lord is coming upon you for a very distinct purpose. I'm filling your earthly body with a spirit of the heavenly, and you will bring heaven into Earth; you will bring God where the devil has been; you will bring Christ where the spirit of Antichrist has been; you will bring the gospel where there has only been bad news. And even now," says the Lord, "I am clothing you with divine purpose [so] that you will reap the harvest. This is your due season. Do not think the harvest will come to you. You must go to the harvest. Do not think the harvest will come to the door. You must take the door to the harvest."

—PHIL PRINGLE
SEPTEMBER 14, 2003

TIME TO REFLECT

- How do you apply this statement to yourself? "A forceful woman advances the kingdom of God."
- This chapter poses the question, Why must we rise? Compile some thoughts together on how you would answer this question.
- How do you apply the prophetic messages that have been spoken this century to your own life?
  The river
  The walls are coming down
  Seven spheres of influence
  God is raising an army

TIME TO ACT

- Where and who is your "crop" to harvest?

bolder, brighter lights

Chapter Five

LIGHTS OFF OR ON; DIM OR BRIGHT?

You are the light of the world. A city on a hill cannot be hidden. Neither do people light a lamp and put it under a bowl. Instead they put it on its stand, and it gives light to everyone in the house. In the same way, let your light shine before men, that they may see your good deeds and praise your Father in heaven.

—Matthew 5:14–16

This scripture, as I've previously mentioned, is one of the foundations upon which the message of this book has been built. I remember my reaction when God first revealed this passage to me. I had mixed emotions. I was excited because I saw the potential in God's vision. I saw confident women impacting and influencing others. I saw light powerfully dispelling the darkness. I also felt an overwhelming sense of sorrow and burden. I believe that for a moment God allowed me to glimpse His grieving heart.

If we are the light of the world, then we are like a city on a hill or a lamp on a stand that gives light to a room. These symbolic pictures are visions and challenges to us as women. If we are going to be the light of the world, then we need to be women who will stand out and be noticed. We need to be bold and confident.

Jesus asserts, though, in this passage that some lights are ineffective because they have been hidden and covered. These lights have been placed under bowls and beds (Luke 8:16) rather than on a stand in the middle of the room.

I believe that God is sad because He sees and He knows that the lives of many women are partly hidden or covered.

God is grieving for His daughters. He sees them covered, and He feels their fears. He sees women hiding, and He feels their insecurities. He sees women imprisoned, and He feels their pain. He sees their locked-up potential, and He feels their frustration.

> *No one lights a lamp and hides it in a jar or puts it under a bed. Instead, he puts it on a stand, so that those who come in can see the light. For there is nothing hidden that will not be disclosed, and nothing concealed that will not be known or brought out into the open.*
> —LUKE 8:16–17

I believe that we are in a God-appointed time when what has been hidden and concealed in the lives of women will be revealed and released. Now is the time for women to be set free and fully realize their dreams and desires, their purpose and potential.

WHAT IS THE STRENGTH OF YOUR LIGHT?

There are different modes in which lights function, and these can represent the different conditions that impact the lives of women and their potential to shine and be an influence.

We need to recognize the strength of our own lights and if we need to turn them on or turn them up so that our lights and our lives will become bolder and brighter.

Condition 1: Lights Off, as They Are Asleep

Lights that are off describe women who are asleep. Their light is not shining; they are not reflecting the life and love of God or impacting or influencing others.

There were times throughout the Bible when God called His people to awaken because they had fallen asleep.

> *Awake, awake! Clothe yourself with strength, O arm of the LORD; awake, as in days gone by, as in generations of old.*
> —ISAIAH 51:9

> *Awake, awake, O Zion, clothe yourself with strength. Put on your garments of splendor, O Jerusalem, the holy city. The uncircumcised*

and defiled will not enter you again. Shake off your dust; rise up, sit enthroned, O Jerusalem.

—ISAIAH 52:1–2

People can be slumbering for a number of reasons. I believe the devil has a potent sleeping tablet called complacency that causes people to be lulled into a false sense of security and contentment. The Bible says that the pressures of life and the pursuit of pleasures can distract and dull us to the things of God (Luke 8:1–15). In dealing with the here-and-now, natural world, we can forget the bigger picture of eternity and the supernatural realm. We can become weary, lazy, or indifferent to God and to fulfilling the responsibilities we have as Christians. These are strong words from the prophet Isaiah:

You women who are so complacent, rise up and listen to me; you daughters who feel secure, hear what I have to say!

—ISAIAH 32:9

Sometimes it is necessary to be prodded by God to stay awake and keep alert. God often prompts me to keep an eternal perspective, remembering that our lives are so short but our eternity is forever. In the quest to raise a family, buy a home, pursue a career, and enjoy all life has to offer, we can sometimes forget there is a heaven—or hell—waiting for us all. We must keep our hearts stirred and our eyes fixed on heaven and who and what we will bring there. In the end, that is all that really matters.

As a pastor, I have also seen people "fall asleep" due to disappointment, discouragement, or disillusionment. They have been numbed by a painful or challenging experience. When we go through confusing or difficult times, we can shut ourselves off from God. Our hearts can feel battered and bruised and our faith disenchanted. We dare not hope again, believe again, or serve again. Our heart stays hurt or, worse, becomes bitter and angry. As a consequence, we can "fall asleep" into an emotional and spiritual stupor.

Thus, before we can arise, we need to make sure we are awake. Most mornings my alarm clock noisily wakes me up, prompting me to rise. Today I am going to be your alarm clock and ask you the question, Are you awake? To become awake again with our lights switched on, we need to repent of complacency and allow our hearts to be healed and revived by God.

Condition 2: Lights Dim Because They Are Hidden

The passage we read earlier in Luke implies that it is ludicrous to hide a light under a bed, because its effectiveness is radically reduced. Sadly, I believe many women have hindered their influence by living "under their bed" to some degree or another. They hide because they lack confidence. They hide because they are scared. They hide because they don't value themselves.

When I was a little girl I would literally retreat under my bed, mostly when I was in trouble or when I wanted to be alone. Because it was a small place, it made me feel safe and secure. No one ever put me under my bed. It was my own decision to retreat to my hiding place. It was also my decision to venture back out. There may be areas in your life in which you, too, are hiding, places you have stayed because they are safe and secure.

Sometimes we hide behind ourselves; other times we hide behind our responsibilities, such as being a mother or a wife; and at other times we hide behind stronger people, such as our husbands, parents, friends, or work colleagues. But I know that God is calling us to venture out from these small spaces into bigger and broader places. To do this we must grow and rise up.

Condition 3: Lights Dim Because They Are Covered

Lights can also be covered by a bowl or hidden in a jar. I believe this refers to the impact that other people can have on our lives. It is possible for women to be living in environments where they are hindered or even blocked from rising and reaching their full potential. I also believe that the devil himself has a vendetta against women becoming free and significant.

At the time the Gospels were written, there was no electricity, so oil burners were used. The light came from a flame that burnt a wick that had been immersed in olive oil. For the flame to continue burning, it required adequate oxygen. If the oil-burner was placed in a jar or covered by a bowl, not only would the light be dimmed, but the flame would eventually be snuffed out, as all the available oxygen would be used up.

Some women find themselves surrounded by circumstances, customs, or people that are like these bowls or jars. These women have been covered, hidden, or hindered. Some of you may even feel like your light and your life have been extinguished by others. In forthcoming chapters we will look at the people and cultures that have tried to conceal women and the demonic onslaught we can face when we choose to rise.

Condition 4: Lights On, Shining Brightly and Boldly

Our aim is to be like this fourth light: a light that is standing upright, switched on, and shining brightly. This image of the light on a stand is one to which we can aspire. It portrays a bold, confident woman who knows who she is and what she is called to do. She is being raised and released by others. She is fighting and defying the devil. She is strong and steadfast. She is brave and courageous. She is standing up and stepping out. She is extraordinary. She is a woman of influence.

THE POWER OF POTENTIAL

Consult not your fears but your hopes and your dreams. Think not about your frustrations, but about your unfulfilled potential. Concern yourself not with what you tried and failed in, but with what it is still possible for you to do.

—POPE JOHN XXIII (1881–1963)[1]

The word *potential* makes me think of…

- a flower that has not yet bloomed,
- the smoldering embers in a fire,
- a seed waiting to germinate,
- the sun rising in the morning,
- a caterpillar in a chrysalis,
- a champagne bottle still corked,
- sails ready to catch the wind,
- and a light switch not turned on.

Potential is a force that is laying dormant—unexpressed and underdeveloped—waiting to be released. Here are some thoughts about the potential that lies within you and me.

Capability not yet apprehended.
Possibility not yet realized.
Capacity not yet produced.
Creativity not yet displayed.
Growth not yet developed.
Action not yet initiated.
Desire not yet fulfilled.
Talent not yet revealed.
Gifts not yet manifested.
Passion not yet expressed.
Goals not yet achieved.
Dreams not yet accomplished.

The word *yet* is small but powerful. It reflects the power of potential, the power of possibility, and the power of decision. *Yet* is the voice that says it can happen. *Yet* is the door which brings promise into reality. *Yet* is the bridge between what is and what can be. *Yet* is the challenge that demands us to rise.

I believe most of us live with unfulfilled potential. We have limited who we can be and what we can do. We have capabilities and possibilities waiting to be released. The images we see in the Scriptures of these dimmed lights are a vivid reminder of potential that is yet to shine. A woman who chooses to rise will make conscious decisions to explore and pursue her dormant gifts, dreams, desires, passions, creativity, and talents. For this to happen she must step courageously from the small, safe, and secure spaces of her life into the broader, bolder, and bigger places. When she does this she will see the "not yet" removed and her potential realized.

We are going to look in more detail at what keeps our lights dim and how we can make our lights bolder and brighter. Our focus will be on the second and third lights that have been introduced in this chapter: lights and lives that are dim because they are hidden or covered. We will look at the internal issues of self confidence and fear, and then recognize the external influences that have kept our potential suppressed or imprisoned. The last chapter in Part Two focuses on what happens when God Himself is restraining us.

TIME TO REFLECT

- Which of the four lights represents your life? Why did you choose this light?
- Draw what your light looks like.
- Are you awake to God and His plan for your life? Is there anything in your life that has caused you to become complacent or weary?
- What potential is yet to be released in your life?
- What would you need to do to make your light shine bolder and brighter?

Chapter Six

RECLAIMING SELF

When I first started life-coaching, I questioned God as to the purpose and mission of my business and the role I was to play as a life coach. He responded by showing me a picture of a woman, with a particular focus on the area around her heart. I saw strong prison bars and a door with a large padlock on her heart; it was caged and captive. I saw a heart full of potential, but it was trapped. I saw purpose waiting to escape, but it was restrained. I sensed God grieving because the gifts and call in many women's lives are not being fully realized and released.

Next I saw God placing in my hands a set of keys. They were large, clanking, old-fashioned keys, each one of them different. I searched through them until I found the key that unlocked the gate surrounding this woman's heart. I positioned and turned the key in the lock. The prison door swung open, and the woman was set free!

I am certain that God is hungry to see the hearts of women unlocked. I believe this is extremely important to Him, because when we are locked, so is He. His purposes on this Earth are limited and hindered when we are imprisoned. When we experience freedom and fulfill our call, the purposes of God can be fully accomplished.

It's worthwhile, then, asking these questions: What are the prison bars? and, What causes women to be held captive? I am convinced that it is largely due to poor self-esteem and the struggles many women face with feelings of vulnerability and insecurity. Self-confidence is the key that will unlock the prison gates and set our hearts free. My definition of *self-confidence* is "the assurance and belief in yourself and your own abilities."

Your self-confidence and self-esteem are tightly interwoven, and they will increase as you focus and strengthen the other areas of self.

- **Self-Identity:** The recognition and acceptance of your unique personality and purpose.
- **Self-Worth:** The respect and appreciation you have for yourself as a precious and capable individual.
- **Self-Image:** The view or perception you hold of your value, appearance, and abilities.
- **Self-Actualization:** The realizing of your potential to develop as a mature, independent, and gifted individual.

I have been a Christian for over twenty years, and I've walked a long journey of personal self-growth. Throughout this chapter I will share with you some of the insights that God has given me along the way. My prayer is that my revelations will become your revelations, that the truth I have encountered you also will encounter. God desires His women to be free, and freedom comes through accepting and applying His truth. The greater the freedom we have, the bolder and brighter will our lights shine.

REVELATION 1: GOD IS MY MAKER

At the moment you accepted Jesus into your life and acknowledged His death and resurrection, you had a revelation of Jesus as your Savior. If you then surrendered your life totally to Him, you should also understand what it means to have Jesus as your Lord. But have you ever pondered the notion that God is your Maker? The Bible says:

> *He is the image of the invisible God, the firstborn over all creation. For by him all things were created: things in heaven and on earth, visible and invisible, whether thrones or powers or rulers or authorities; all things were created by him and for him.*
>
> —COLOSSIANS 1:15–16

Everything is created by Jesus and everything is created for Jesus. What a big statement! I want you to pause for a moment and personalize this truth by writing your name in the space below.

- I, _____, am created by God, and
- I, _____, am created for God.

Colossians 1:15–16 tells you and me that our identity and purpose are found in God and in Him alone. It informs us of our origin and our destiny. When we grasp the fact that we have been created by God and that He is our Maker, we are able to answer the big questions of life:

- **Identity:** Who am I?
- **Purpose:** Why am I here?
- **Origin:** Where have I come from?
- **Destiny:** Where am I going?

Read these truths aloud:

I was made by the Maker. I did not evolve from monkeys or apes. I was not a mistake or born by chance. I was created by God. He dreamt about me before I was even conceived. He designed me with my unique looks, passions, skills, and personality. He fashioned me with His hands. I am special and significant. I am precious and valuable. I have been made with specific intent. I have a purpose to fulfill on this earth. God has plans for my life that are extraordinary. When I die heaven will be my home and I will live with Jesus forever.

When God is described in the Bible as the Maker it is often with a capital *M*, which often denotes a title or a position. This means that God is the preeminent Maker. He is the greatest, the most excellent Maker, and His skill is unrivalled and incomparable. He is the Master Craftsman, and that means we are His masterpiece. Spend a moment reflecting on the process and different stages you go through when you create something, whether it is cooking, painting, designing clothes, gardening, renovating, or building a home. The steps involved with being creative are universal.

I'm sure you'd agree that the first stage of creating something is always vision. Before you begin it is necessary to have some idea of the finished product. In your imagination you are able to see the form, shape, and function of your handiwork. It is common at this stage to be filled with energy and excitement. The next stage is researching and planning, the how and what you will need to complete your project. Then you progress to the hands-on phase, when you actually get out your raw materials and start to cut, paint, cook, sew, or hammer. This is the time when you get your hands dirty. The final stage is showing off your finished product. This is the phase where you will experience a sense of achievement and satisfaction because of the wonderful work you have created.

Just think, God went through all these steps when He created you. He took time to reflect upon all your special features and functions. He dreamt of you. He carried you in His heart and mind. He was excited about you. Even before you were here, you brought Him joy and delight. Then He began to make you with His very own hands. The Bible says, "Yet, O LORD, you are our Father. We are the clay, you are the potter; we are all the work of your hand" (Isa. 64:8). What a wonderful image: God with His hands wrapped all around the clay, sculpturing every intricate part of you. Finally He finishes and says to you, His creation, "How wonderful you are!"

Potters design many different pots. Each one is made according to the shape most appropriate for fulfilling a specific purpose. So it is with you and me. We are God's vessels created for His purpose—and His pleasure. Before we were conceived, God had dreamt and planned what shape we would be and what function we would perform. He knew the purpose He intended for us to fulfill here on Earth. In the process of creating, He placed within us our own unique call, personality, and talents. Three men in the Old Testament, David, Jeremiah, and Isaiah, each had a revelation of how special they were and how and why they were created by God.

> *For you created my inmost being; you knit me together in my mother's womb. I praise you because I am fearfully and wonderfully made; your works are wonderful, I know that full well. My frame was not hidden from you when I was made in the secret place. When I was woven together in the depths of the earth, your eyes saw my unformed body. All the days ordained for me were written in your book before one of them came to be.*
> —PSALM 139:13–16, A PSALM OF KING DAVID

> *The word of the LORD came to me, saying, "Before I formed you in the womb I knew you, before you were born I set you apart; I appointed you as a prophet to the nations."*
> —JEREMIAH 1:4–5

Before I was born the LORD *called me; from my birth he has made mention of my name.*

—ISAIAH 49:1

Before we were even conceived God knew us and called us. We were set apart for a divine purpose from the beginning of our existence. Whilst we were growing in our mother's womb, God was beautifully knitting us together. And, as my girlfriend once said to me, "God doesn't drop stitches!" He designed and created everything about us: our body, face, personality, passions, desires, talents, and gifts. He could see all the days ahead of us before we had even drawn our first breath. He even knew our name!

I have felt prompted lately to speak to women about these words of David: "I praise you because I am fearfully and wonderfully made; your works are wonderful, I know that full well" (Psalm 139:14). I am convinced that if every person could believe and speak these words over their life, they would be transformed. We need to be able to exclaim with complete boldness and assurance, "I praise you, God, because I fully realize that I am wonderful! I am an extraordinary piece of your handiwork! You have made me, and you have done an amazing job. I thank you and applaud you!"

The following two scriptures contain not gentle words from God, but rather a rebuke.

But who are you, O man, to talk back to God? "Shall what is formed say to him who formed it, 'Why did you make me like this?'" Does not the potter have the right to make out of the same lump of clay some pottery for noble purposes and some for common use?

—ROMANS 9:20–21

"Woe to him who quarrels with his Maker, to him who is but a potsherd among the potsherds on the ground. Does the clay say to the potter, 'What are you making?' Does your work say, 'He has no hands'? Woe to him who says to his father, 'What have you begotten?' or to his mother, 'What have you brought to birth?'"

—ISAIAH 45:9–10

God reminds us through this reprimand that it is not our place to question Him about who we are and how we were made. God did not get it wrong or do a half-hearted job when He created us. We are exactly what He wanted and what He needed. It is important that we acknowledge God as our Maker and accept that we have been designed and created by Him. I know that as individuals do this, they will discover a new sense of peace and liberty.

REVELATION 2: IMAGE BROKEN

At the beginning of the Bible we read that men and women were created in God's image and likeness. The Scriptures say, "Let us make man in our image, in our likeness" (Gen. 1:26–27). To whom does *us* and *our* refer? I believe we have a lovely picture here of the Trinity of God—the Father, Son, and Holy Spirit—meeting and discussing the design and creation of humankind. Together they decided that man and woman would be made in their image.

Isn't it amazing? We are created with a resemblance or similarity to God!

There are facets of the nature and character of the Godhead that are mirrored in all humans. This can be seen in the ability of people to be creative; to operate in faith; to show mercy, grace, and forgiveness; to have an intellect with which to think and reason; and to express love and friendship in relationships. We have also been created with a will, emotions, and a spirit. Inherent in humans is the authority to rule and be fruitful. We were so wonderfully created that even God was impressed. When He finished His masterpiece and the pinnacle of all that He created, He exclaimed that it was very good!

The fall of mankind, however, brought dire consequences to God's creation. When Adam and Eve chose to disobey God (Gen. 3), sin entered the world, and humankind was radically changed forever. Immediately the image was broken. No longer did we fully reflect God, but we became marred and influenced by the one who sought to deceive and destroy us. Now, we reflected some of the devil's image and attributes: selfishness, pride, arrogance, envy, and jealousy. We were also left with feelings of guilt and shame. And, most significantly, we became separated from God. This is why Jesus had to come and die for us. He came to redeem what had been destroyed. He came to mend our relationship with Him and restore our broken image.

Because of sin and the fall of mankind, we now live in an imperfect world and are confronted every day with situations that can damage us. It is probable that we already have been, and will continue to be, affected by tragedy, sickness, abuse, or dysfunctional relationships. These have resulted in the symptoms of a fallen world: pain, grief, sorrow, insecurities, shame, rejection, vulnerability and addictions. The devil has made it his personal mission to destroy our self-image and our self-worth. We, therefore, must be on a personal mission to reclaim what has been stolen, to once again know how beautiful and wonderful we are and how powerful we can be.

REVELATION 3: GOD HAS MADE ME AND IS MAKING ME

I want you to realize this simple and profound truth:

You have been made, but you are still being made!

Until the day we die, we are in a continual process of being transformed, shaped, and molded by God. The image that was broken and damaged is on a journey of being restored and made strong again. We are all what I would call works in progress. Let me share one of my favorite scriptures:

I reflect the Lord's glory and am being transformed by the Holy Spirit to be more like Jesus. I will continue to grow from glory to glory, shining Jesus a little brighter every day!
—2 CORINTHIANS 3:18, AUTHOR'S PARAPHRASE

The word *transformed* in this scripture comes from the Greek word *metamorphoo*, from which we get the word "metamorphosis." This process of personal transformation is similar to the journey a caterpillar makes to become a beautiful butterfly. That's us, ladies! We are changing little by little through the power of the Holy Spirit to be more like Jesus. The other thing I love about the word *transformation* is that it literally means "to change into another form." That suggests we are not just going to be a wee bit different but radically and totally changed.

MY STORY

Even though I will experience a transformation process until the day I die, I personally went through an intensive time of metamorphosis when I had to deal with my insecurities and my pain. This journey of healing began for me at the end of 1998, the year God called me to rise up. I began 1999 with the same simple question I ask God every New Year, What is my word for this year?

The reply?

"This is your year to grow up!"

Wow! That answer took me completely by surprise! After having such an amazing year filled with vision and enlargement, now I had to grow up. At first I felt offended. "What am I doing that is not grown up?" I wondered. Then I felt a little scared, because deep down I had a sense of what this growing up process would entail.

I felt led to this scripture:

> *When I was a child, I talked like a child, I thought like a child, I reasoned like a child. When I became a man, I put childish ways behind me.*
> —1 CORINTHIANS 13:11

God impressed upon me this statement: "I don't want you to be a girl in God; I want you to be a woman of God."

It's important to realize that no matter what our age, you and I will always be daughters and children of God, just like we are daughters and children to our natural parents. As we physically grow up and become women with adult responsibilities, we also need to grow up in our spiritual life and our relationship with our heavenly Father. We cannot remain as young children of God. Rather, we need to grow in maturity and become God's adult children. His dream is that His girls will develop into strong, responsible, dignified women. I have learned that this does not happen overnight. It's a long and, at times, arduous journey.

So at the age of thirty-six I began growing up in the areas in my world that were weak and vulnerable. Without a doubt they were the most difficult years of my life. For six months I could not stop crying. Almost every Sunday I would go to church and weep. At times this was incredibly uncomfortable to have my emotions so publicly visible. As a pastor, I felt a pressure to have my life all together. But I chose to ignore my own and other people's opinions and be humble before my God. I knew only in Him would I find my healing and my freedom.

There were times when I would go out for prayer at healing altar calls, and there were other occasions when I wept uncontrollably in the arms of my husband or a friend. Thankfully, they knew that they didn't have to give me answers or solutions. They allowed me just to cry! In crying there was release and freedom. At times I didn't even know why I was crying. The intensity of my sobs actually overwhelmed me. They came from somewhere so deep inside of me. It felt like God was opening the door of a hidden, tightly-closed room in my heart. Even I was not aware that the pain had been hiding there.

During those years I sought the wisdom of counselors, the prayers of my pastor, and the support of my husband and a couple of close friends. And of course, I held on to God. When I go through different seasons in my life, I have learned to ask God for a word or a picture to show me what He is doing and why. These words and pictures always give me insight, encouragement, and faith. God gave me two scriptures during this season of healing, and I held on to them with everything I had. They were His promises to me. They provided me with clarity and understanding, but also faith, hope, and vision.

> *This is the word that came to Jeremiah from the LORD: "Go down to the potter's house, and there I will give you my message." So I went down to the potter's house, and I saw him working at the wheel. But the pot he was shaping from the clay was marred in his hands; so the potter formed it into another pot, shaping it as seemed best to him*
> —JEREMIAH 18:1–4

This word was my first promise. Through this scripture, God showed me both what He was doing and why. I was a marred pot. This word *marred* means "blemished, flawed, disfigured, and spoiled." I don't know if you have ever had the experience of shaping clay on a potter's wheel, but it is an extremely difficult thing to do. If you do not center the clay correctly on the wheel, you will make a very lopsided, misshapen pot. Well, guess what? That was me. God showed me that my foundations were flawed, so I was "wonky." He was going to have to rebuild my inner foundations so that I could be whole and healthy, a pot that would be strong and useful.

> *Blessed are those whose strength is in you, who have set their hearts on pilgrimage. As they pass through the Valley of Baca, they make it a place of springs; the autumn rains also cover it with pools. They go from strength to strength, till each appears before God in Zion.*
> —PSALM 84:5–7

This passage was my second promise from God. It was an assurance that I would pass through this valley and that the journey would have an end. I desperately needed to know this, because there were times when I thought that it would never finish. I have found that when God deals with an area in your heart and you think you have come to a time when it is finished, He sometimes then takes you a little deeper—and then even deeper still. This process can take months, sometimes even years. My counselor gave me some wise advice that I have passed on to many others going through a similar season. She said that the pain in your heart is in layers, like an onion, and that God can't go straight to the core because it would be too painful. He works from the outside in, healing a little at a time.

This scripture mentions passing through the Valley of Baca, or the Valley of Weeping. Here was another promise that all the tears I had been weeping would at some stage come to an end. I was also encouraged that the healing of my heart was called a pilgrimage, a deliberate and sacred journey I chose to take. I was being transformed along the way, and it would take me to my future. I was indeed growing from strength to strength, from glory to glory.

The Book of Isaiah has some interesting scriptures regarding our past. I have discovered that you cannot move forward into your future until you have dealt with the pain from your past.

Tell us what the former things were, so that we may consider them and know their final outcome.

—Isaiah 41:22

Forget the former things; do not dwell on the past. See, I am doing a new thing! Now it springs up; do you not perceive it? I am making a way in the desert and streams in the wasteland.

—Isaiah 43:18–19

Before the new thing can happen in your life, the painful events of the past need to be identified and the consequences considered. Only then can they be forgotten and no longer dwelt upon. You may need to seek counseling, have someone pray for you, and perhaps cry a few (or many) tears. It will definitely be necessary for you to forgive; possibly repent; and to nail every pain, torment, insecurity, sorrow, or grief to the cross of Jesus.

If God directs you to deal with an area in your life that is weak, fragile, or broken, be brave and go through this journey of restoration. It is painful. You do need to be strong and courageous. But I assure you that through the valley, on the other side, there is freedom. Just keep walking. Don't turn back. The previous scripture from Isaiah says that streams will flow in the places where there was desert and wasteland. I love this imagery. Whatever your desert is now, God will transform it into a spring or a fertile, lush field. This is metamorphosis: total change from one form to another.

I will make rivers flow on barren heights, and springs within the valleys. I will turn the desert into pools of water, and the parched ground into springs. I will put in the desert the cedar and the acacia, the myrtle and the olive. I will set pines in the wasteland, the fir and the cypress together, so that people may see and know, may consider and understand, that the hand of the Lord has done this, that the Holy One of Israel has created it.

—Isaiah 41:18–20

This theme is also highlighted in another passage in Isaiah:

Till the Spirit is poured upon us from on high, and the desert becomes a fertile field, and the fertile field seems like a forest. Justice will dwell in the desert and righteousness live in the fertile field. The fruit of righteousness will be peace; the effect of righteousness will be quietness and confidence forever.

—Isaiah 32:15–17

What a beautiful promise to hold on to: that the areas in our life that are barren, weak, and broken can be made fruitful, strong, and whole. The Lord who created you can also recreate you. The precious Holy Spirit will bring about this supernatural transformation. When this change occurs in our lives, justice will reign and righteousness will be restored. Our lives will display a deep inner peace and self-confidence.

REVELATION 4: DISCOVERING SELF

I believe every person is special and significant. We have each been created by God with a unique identity and purpose. I believe that when we are armed with this self-awareness, then we become more confident and capable. Without this knowledge and understanding, we can feel uncertain and lost. The ancient Greek philosopher Socrates put it this way: "Know thyself."

Author Costa Mitchell says:

> *Being ignorant about who you are leaves you with pain of uncertainty, questioning your reason for existence, and unable to answer the questions.*[1]

In my own journey of restoring my self-image and self-worth, I sought to understand not only that I am special and significant but rather how am I special and how my life is significant. I was hungry for these answers. I came to the conclusion that if God dreamt about me, designed me, and created me, then He should be the one who knows and can tell me the answers to these questions. So I sought God!

During one of these times when I was seeking Him, I found myself pondering some questions about Jesus. I was thinking, Did Jesus have a healthy self-image? What did He know about His own unique identity and purpose? As I searched the Gospel of John, I discovered that Jesus often made bold statements about Himself. He also knew the answers to the four big questions of life: Where have I come from? Who am I? What am I called to do? Where am I going?

There is one story in particular that I love about Jesus. It shows us how secure and confident He was in Himself. He knew His past, His future, and His mission. He also understood the appointed times and purposes of God. Armed with this knowledge, Jesus was able to become a servant to His disciples and demonstrate fully His love for them. This is the fruit of strong self-esteem and self-confidence. When you know who you are, you don't have to fight for position, power, or prestige. You can simply serve. Let's look at the story. As you read, notice what Jesus did because of what He knew.

> It was just before the Passover Feast. Jesus knew that the time had come for him to leave this world and go to the Father. Having loved his own who were in the world, he now showed them the full extent of his love. The evening meal was being served, and the devil had already prompted Judas Iscariot, son of Simon, to betray Jesus. Jesus knew that the Father had put all things under his power, and that he had come from God and was returning to God; so he got up from the meal, took off his outer clothing, and wrapped a towel around his waist. After that, he poured water into a basin and began to wash his disciples' feet, drying them with the towel that was wrapped around him.
>
> —JOHN 13:1–5

The Gospel of John records many of Jesus' bold statements about Himself, revelations I believe He received during time spent with His Father. I have come to call these declarations "Jesus' I ams." Jesus made seven "I am" statements in the Gospel of John.

- "I am the bread of life" (John 6:35).
- "I am the light of the world" (John 8:12).
- "I am the gate for the sheep" (John 10:7).
- "I am the good shepherd" (John 10:11).
- "I am the resurrection and the life" (John 11:25).

- "I am the way and the truth and the life" (John 14:6).
- "I am the true vine" (John 15:1, 5).

Each one of these statements reveals to us something about the character and purpose of Jesus. They provide an image that symbolizes a certain aspect of Jesus' nature and His ministry. From these "I ams" we can see that Jesus understood who He was and what He was called to do. Indeed, Jesus' self-image was very strong and healthy. Let's look at two of Jesus' "I am" statements.

Jesus described Himself as a good shepherd. This was a profession and a responsibility that would have been commonly understood by the people to whom Jesus first spoke these words. In Bible times, a shepherd attended to the needs of his flock of sheep. To satisfy the hunger and thirst of the sheep, he would find lush, green pastures and fresh, calm water. He would lead the flock by talking to the sheep, and the sheep would follow his voice. At times the shepherd would be required to protect his sheep from predators, such as wolves, bears, and lions. A good shepherd would risk his own life to save his precious sheep. This image gives us a clear picture of who Jesus is and what He was called to do. We can know that Jesus loves us, knows us, talks to us, guides us, protects us, and cares for us. Most significantly, we know that Jesus sacrificed His own life to save us.

Let's look at one more example. Jesus said, "I am the bread of life" (John 6:35). Bread was the staple food of the Jewish people. It provided the main means for satisfying hunger and providing nourishment and sustenance to their bodies. Put simply, bread was essential for life. Jesus said about Himself, "I am the living bread that came down from heaven. If anyone eats of this bread, he will live forever. This bread is my flesh, which I will give for the life of the world" (John 6:51). This image reminds us that it is only Jesus who can provide the spiritual food that will nourish and sustain our life, now and for all eternity.

Jesus had at least seven different "I ams," and I believe our Father in heaven wants to give you and me our own personal "I ams." I would like to share with you my story of one of my "I ams" in the hope that you will seek God for your own. I have found that these images from God often reveal something about both our strengths and our weaknesses. It's important, then, that you pray for the correct interpretation of any image or words you receive. The picture will enlighten you, encourage you, challenge you, and even possibly warn you.

Many years ago I asked God to reveal to me a picture of His thoughts about me. Straight away I saw the image of a sunflower. I have since taken many photos of these flowers and have discovered lots of wonderful things about them. In the process, I have been able to learn things about my own identity and purpose.

If God sees me as a sunflower, I know some things to be true about myself. I am happy, colorful, bold, and beautiful. I stand tall, strong, and dignified. I shine brightly, and I follow the Son as He moves across the sky. But sunflowers are large, singular flowers that stand alone. This can leave them open and vulnerable to harsh elements, such as excessive heat or strong winds. This reinforced to me that as a leader I have at times felt exposed and open to demonic attack.

A number of months after this first experience God reminded me of the sunflower. He asked me, "What products do you get from a sunflower?" I thought for a moment and answered, "You get seeds and oil." He replied with these words: "Yes, that's right. And this is what I have called you to minister." Immediately I understood what He was saying. I was to minister both His Word (sunflower seeds) and the Holy Spirit (sunflower oil). God was showing me that He would equip and anoint me to be a minister who could effectively preach and teach the Word of God and also pray for people so they would be touched by the presence of His Spirit. This was such an encouraging revelation.

Since then God has given me a number of different "I ams." He has shown me that I am a warrior, a thoroughbred horse, and a messenger. Each revelation is rich and very personal. It gives me a snapshot of who I am and what God has called me to do. It provides an encouragement from the Father who created me about my own unique identity and purpose.

The Bible says that we are living in the days when we can all prophesy (Acts 2:17–18). That means everyone can see and hear messages from God. Often we apply this verse to our ability to prophesy words over other people, but I have discovered that God wants us to receive prophecies direct from heaven for our own lives. Let me encourage you today to ask God to reveal something to you about yourself. It may just astound you!

> However, as it is written: "No eye has seen, no ear has heard, no mind has conceived what God has prepared for those who love him"—but God has revealed it to us by his Spirit. The Spirit searches all things, even the deep things of God.
>
> —1 Corinthians 2:9–10

Revelation 5: No Comparison

The prophet John the Baptist is an inspiration to me. He is a man who knew his identity and purpose. He not only recognized who he was but also—and very importantly—who he was not. This knowledge gave him confidence, freedom, and authority. I have found many women battle with comparing themselves to others and wishing they were something or someone else. John could boldly say both "I am" and "I am not" statements. It is just as powerful to discover who and what you are not as it is to find out who and what you are! Let's have a look at some scriptures about John and what he said about himself.

> There came a man who was sent from God; his name was John. He came as a witness to testify concerning that light, so that through him all men might believe. He himself was not the light; he came only as a witness to the light. The true light that gives light to every man was coming into the world.
>
> —John 1:6–9

> Now this was John's testimony when the Jews of Jerusalem sent priests and Levites to ask him who he was. He did not fail to confess, but confessed freely, "I am not the Christ." They asked him, "Then who are you? Are you Elijah?" He said, "I am not." "Are you the Prophet?" He answered, "No." Finally they said, "Who are you? Give us an answer to take back to those who sent us. What do you say about yourself?" John replied in the words of Isaiah the prophet, "I am the voice of one calling in the desert, 'Make straight the way for the Lord.'"
>
> —John 1:19–23

Many times in life we can be hampered and challenged by the success of peers or people close to us. John the Baptist was not like this. He had a clear understanding of his own identity and purpose; therefore, he was able to recognize and release others into the fullness of their own call. An example of this is found in John 1:35–37. John is with two of his disciples when Jesus happens to walk past. John finds himself prophesying, "Look, the Lamb of God!" (v. 36). Immediately, John's two disciples leave him to follow Jesus and become His disciples. I believe that many people would feel threatened by an incident like this. Not John. He neither compared himself to Jesus, nor was he jealous. He remained strong and secure, his self-worth unshaken.

REVELATION 6: GOD'S PROMISE TO HIS WOMEN

One cold winter's day I was sitting in one of my favorite spots, in front of the heater. I was reading my Bible, and I had what I could only call an encounter with God. It felt like God visited me. He quickened to my spirit what I was reading from the Book of Isaiah. I believe the words from this passage of scripture are extremely significant. They provide yet another of the foundational stones upon which the message of this book has been built.

I am convinced this passage is a prophetic promise being spoken by God to His daughters. He is declaring today, "For your sake, for the sake of all women, for the sake of my church, and for the sake of my kingdom, I want and need my daughters to be set free. My desire is to see your righteousness shine and your glory influence the lives of many. I want you to know you are beautifully loved and highly capable. You are a royal princess who holds authority and favor within your hand. And until this happens I will not keep quiet and I will not stop fighting for you."

For Zion's sake I will not keep silent, for Jerusalem's sake I will not remain quiet, till her righteousness shines out like the dawn, her salvation like a blazing torch. The nations will see your righteousness, and all kings your glory; you will be called by a new name that the mouth of the LORD will bestow. You will be a crown of splendor in the LORD's hand, a royal diadem in the hand of your God. No longer will they call you Deserted, or name your land Desolate. But you will be called

*Hephzibah, and your land Beulah; for the L*ORD *will take delight in you, and your land will be married.*

—I<small>SAIAH</small> 62:1–4

This passage is filled with promise and purpose. The verses focus on the themes of shining and being an influence. Isaiah is also declaring in this prophecy that women will see radical transformation in their lives. He claims that the changes will be so profound that we will actually be given a new name and a new land to live in.

Isaiah has declared, "No longer will women be named 'Deserted' and live in the land called 'Desolate.'" These names reflect the beliefs that many women hold in their hearts that they are not loved or have anything to offer. What potent lies of the devil! Let's take a moment to understand from what we are being set free.

- *Deserted* means "rejected, unloved, abandoned, unappreciated, unworthy, forsaken, and isolated."
- *Desolate* means "barren, unfruitful, unproductive, empty, and gloomy."

Here is the promise! Here is the truth! No longer will women feel rejected and insignificant. Rather, they will walk tall, crowned with the revelation of their value and worth. God will give them a new name, "Hephzibah," and a new land to live in, "Beulah."

- *Hephzibah* means "my delight is in her." This name implies she will feel loved, special, precious, cherished, and accepted. Why? Because God delights in, enjoys, rejoices over, takes pleasure in, and is enchanted by her.
- *Beulah* means "married." This name implies a place of relationship that leads to love, security, fruitfulness, productivity, and joy. With marriage comes a home and children. This symbolizes a place of purpose, significance, and fulfillment.

Through this passage of scripture, God is declaring that it's a new day for many women. Today you can know that you are special and significant. You can be assured of these promises: "God absolutely delights in you, and you are 'a crown of splendor in the Lord's hand.'" You can arm yourself with the revelation that you are destined to live a fertile and fruitful life. You are also a woman who carries authority and has the capacity to influence. You can do this gently by shining the love of Jesus like the beautiful rising sun at dawn. Or you can do this powerfully, like a blazing torch taking light into dark places.

I find this quotation very insightful:

> *To develop a positive self-image, a child needs to know two things: I am loved and I am competent.*
>
> —Costa Mitchell[2]

One of my coaching clients reiterated this thought once to me in a slightly different way. She said, "We all need to know that we are lovable and able." I believe God, through Isaiah, is loudly declaring that we are both. We are truly loved and lovable. And yes, we are competent and able to live lives of impact and fruitfulness. As we grow in our knowledge, acceptance, and enjoyment of how and whom God has made us, the greater our lights will shine. Every day they will glow a little more brightly, boldly, and beautifully.

TIME TO REFLECT

- Identify how wonderfully you have been created by listing your unique looks, style, personality, passions, talents, desires, and character attributes.
- Reflect upon the changes that have already taken place in your life since you met God. Identify one area of your world where God is presently "making" you.
- Reflect upon this statement: "I don't want you to be a girl in God; I want you to be a woman of God."
- Spend some time with God and ask Him to show you some "I ams" for your own life. Reflect upon how they portray your unique purpose and personality.
- Have you ever questioned God about how or why He made you? If yes, you need to say sorry and make a decision to accept and thank God for who you are. You can write down this decision by starting with, "Today I choose to accept..."
- Write down some thoughts about who and what you are not.
- Answer these questions:
  My identity: Who am I?
  My purpose: What am I here for?
  My origin: Where have I come from?
  My destiny: Where am I going?

TIME TO ACT

- Do you need to deal with your past? If yes, make an appointment to talk with a trusted friend or a professional counselor.

Chapter Seven

CONFRONTING AND CONQUERING FEAR

One can choose to go back toward safety or forward toward growth.
Growth must be chosen again and again; fear must be overcome again
and again.

—ABRAHAM MASLOW, PSYCHOLOGIST (1908–1970)[1]

In this chapter we will focus on the issues that affect our self-confidence and cause us to retreat and hide, keeping us small, and our lights dim and ineffective. We have looked at how important it is to have a strong sense of self. The second most significant factor that prevents women from rising up and reaching their full potential is fear.

Fear is insidious. It can poison, imprison, and paralyze us. It has the power to affect our entire being. Fear can stop us from dealing with change, facing challenges, and moving forward to embrace our dreams. It's highly likely that at some time in your life you have experienced fear restricting you in some way. I detest fear because it steals my power, leaving me feeling small and insignificant.

Yet fear is a part of who we are. It plays an intrinsic role in our everyday life. The good news is that fear can be a powerful motivating force for change when it is teamed with faith and courage. We actually do have the ability, with God's delivering grace and power, to confront and conquer every fear that stands before us. How I love this declaration by King David:

I sought the LORD, *and he answered me; he delivered me from all my*
fears.

—PSALM 34:4

UNDERSTANDING FEAR

In dealing with my own fears I have found it helpful to understand the physiological and emotional responses that take place in my body when I feel afraid. This knowledge enables me to respond more rationally and to apply practical steps toward overcoming the fear. Let's take a look at some general information about fear: what it is, what causes it, and how our body reacts. Knowledge brings understanding, understanding brings power, and power brings freedom.

What Is Fear?

Fear is a natural response in humans because we are physical beings who can suffer pain, sickness, injury, and death. We are also emotional beings who can experience trauma, failure, shame, abandonment, embarrassment, or rejection. Fear is an inbuilt mechanism that aims to protect us. It is actually linked to our basic drive of self-preservation. When we are confronted with situations that breach our physical safety or emotional security, fear can result.

What Causes Fear?

Fear is often an internal reaction to an external stimulus. The outside forces that can cause fear are many and varied: certain conditions, activities, objects, animals, people, places, or situations. Here are some examples.

- **Conditions:** heights, darkness, confined places, water, noise, death, war
- **Activities:** flying, swimming, driving, working, shopping, using the telephone
- **Objects:** needles, dentist drills, fire, cars, airplanes, machines, bikes
- **Animals:** spiders, snakes, insects, dogs, sharks, horses
- **People:** dentists, doctors, bosses, bullies, abusive people
- **Places:** hospitals, schools, crowds, bridges, tall buildings
- **Situations:** confrontations, making decisions, change, exams, the unknown, illness, commitment, responsibility, public speaking, being alone

Some fears begin internally, from within our heart and mind. They are a reflection of our sense of self, and they affect our ability to cope and be successful in many areas of our lives.

- **Internal:** rejection, success, failure, abandonment, intimacy, helplessness, disapproval, being taken advantage of, loss of image

How Our Body Reacts to Fear

When we meet these real or perceived threats our bodies respond on an emotional and physical level. The responses people have can range from worry and anxiety to more extreme reactions such as panic and terror or even phobias and paranoia.

The symptoms we experience are diverse but common in most cases.

- **Emotional:** anxiety, self-doubt, insecurity, timidity, and despair
- **Physical:** sweating, muscle tension, accelerated heart rate, shortness of breath, dilation of pupils, goose bumps on the skin, dry mouth, dizziness, numbness, nausea, trembling, or shaking

These physical symptoms occur when the body activates what's called the "fight or flight response." When we are facing real or presumed danger our brain releases chemicals such as adrenaline, noradrenalin, and cortisol into our bloodstream. These processes prepare our bodies physically and psychologically to either fight or flee. We will either attack and defend our ground or run as fast and as far from the threat as possible.

When we react to fear with feelings of insecurity and timidity, we are more likely to retreat physically or emotionally ("flight"). On other occasions our immediate reaction is to retaliate ("fight"). Some "fight" responses can cause damage, and for some people they can become addictive. Symptoms of "fighting" can include such things as:

- unreasonable stubbornness
- physical violence
- verbal aggression
- obsessive cleanliness
- extreme competitiveness

- overreaction
- hyper-vigilance
- excessive work
- addiction to risk-seeking pursuits
- need to be in control

The "fight or flight" process is very much an instinctive response. When it happens our thinking can become distorted because our rational mind is bypassed. But this seemingly automatic system can be overridden. We can learn new ways of thinking and responding to the factors or forces that produce fear. We can change the way our bodies react.

TYPES OF FEAR

It's not possible to address every individual fear; however, I want to highlight some that are common and that will give you insight into specific fears of your own.

1. Fear of Objects or Situations

People have weird and wacky fears about all manner of things large and small, legitimately dangerous and harmless, serious and silly. No matter what the object or situation, the feeling of fear is very real, however, and can be extremely debilitating.

When I was a teenager, I had an irrational and uncontrollable fear of one particular creepy-crawly. I vividly remember sitting on my bed studying for an exam when I heard a rustling sound. I turned around to see a large cockroach climbing up between my bed and the wall. My response was instantaneous and irrational. I let out a loud scream, jumped off my bed, and bolted out of my room.

My parents were out that night; only my older sister and her boyfriend were at home. In sheer panic I came running out to them beseeching their help. They exclaimed with a hint of mockery, "It's only a cockroach." Thankfully, they did show me mercy by killing the nasty critter. I was then able to return to my bed, somewhat calmed by the knowledge that my enemy was dead. But my heart was still racing, my nerves were on edge, and my senses were on full alert to any further attacks.

I realized after this event that I had a problem that I needed to deal with. So I asked Pat, who was my boyfriend at the time, to pray with me. I'm not sure if God had ever had anyone pray to Him before about overcoming a fear of cockroaches, but that's what I did!

God's approach to helping me deal with my fears was that I would have to face them. I could not keep running. Two days later I had one of the dreaded creepy-crawlies turn up in my car.

When I first spotted the cockroach on my windshield I was unsure whether it was inside or outside the glass. I desperately hoped that it was on the outside, but after turning on my windshield wipers I realized it was inside the car—with me. I panicked and jumped out of the car. The "flight" response had been activated. I wanted to flee a million miles away.

But I had a problem. There was no one else around to help. I knew that I had to kill the cockroach so I could drive my car again. It would not be good enough just to shoo it away, as it could run and hide somewhere else, only to scare me again at a later time. I had only one choice. I had to exterminate it, and I had to do it now!

I took a few deep breaths, and from the safety of my position outside the car I came up with a plan while keeping a watchful eye on the cockroach. The last thing I wanted was it running into some crack or crevice that I could not possibly reach. I took off my shoe and took careful aim. I could not risk just wounding the cockroach and letting it escape. I dealt the lethal blow, and the cockroach was killed—very squashed and very dead!

Killing one cockroach may seem like a small achievement, but to me it was a great victory. I had faced a fear and conquered it. This fear that had imprisoned me no longer held me captive. I can now see cockroaches and not even flinch. Even more, I get great delight out of stomping on them.

In one of the psalms we read these words of King David:

> *You will not fear the terror of night, nor the arrow that flies by day nor the pestilence that stalks in the darkness, nor the plague that destroys at midday.*
>
> —PSALM 91:5–6

I suspect that David was able to make this declaration with such confidence because he had overcome these very same fears with God's help. As a soldier, David would have known the terror of death and the dread of an enemy being close. In the stillness of the night, David would have seen the menacing shadows and heard the crackle of branches and the rustle of leaves, wondering if it was an animal foraging for food or his enemy waiting to attack. David had learned that God could help him confront and conquer all his fears. God was the one that could save, shield, and shelter him. It was only God that could be his fortress and refuge in the midst of war and the darkness of night.

We are living in an era when natural disasters, war, and terrorism abound. Many people are under constant physical threat and the fear of losing their homes, farms, businesses, friends, family, and even their lives. David also understood these fears. Again we see that he was able to stand upon the revelation that God was his source of protection and help from any calamity that might surround him.

> *God is our refuge and strength, an ever-present help in trouble. Therefore we will not fear, though the earth give way and the mountains fall into the heart of the sea, though its waters roar and foam and the mountains quake with their surging.*
>
> —PSALM 46:1–3

> *Even though I walk through the valley of the shadow of death, I will fear no evil, for you are with me; your rod and your staff, they comfort me.*
>
> —PSALM 23:4

2. Fear of Failure

Fear of failure is extraordinarily powerful and immobilizing because it touches upon many other innate fears that reside in the hearts of people: the fear of rejection, the fear of making mistakes, the fear of looking foolish, and the fear of losing approval. These fears spring from our basic human needs, such as the need to belong, to be loved, to be recognized by others, and to be successful.

For many years I have taught in classrooms as a lecturer and outdoors as an environmental educator. This teaching had taken a toll on my voice, and I sought help from Shelley, an opera singer, who trains people in the correct use of their voice. During my first session she explained how much nervousness plays a role in a person's voice being strained. I realized that my nerves were due to very deep-seated fears. In the past I had learned to push through fear, but now it seemed time to explore the root of the fears. It was no longer time to put on confidence but rather to be confident. For this shift to take place God had to heal my heart of some deep fears of failure and shame.

I left my voice lesson that day knowing that God was wanting to set me free. As I drove home, memories began to surface in my mind, each one a specific event from my past—from childhood to adolescence to adulthood—in which I had experienced failure in a public setting. I remembered the emotional pain that I had felt at these different times, pain I had locked away deep inside of me. In some of the situations I had felt incompetent and useless; in others humiliated, ridiculed, and embarrassed.

I went home and had a big cry. Then I wrote down and made sketches of the different events and the pain I experienced. I prayed through each situation, asking God to deliver me from the effects of these traumatic events in my life.

The occasions ranged from forgetting a message I had to give the principal of my primary school when I was only six years old, to being mocked by my school friends and branded with labels such as "loser" and "boring." The most significant and painful was being reprimanded and ridiculed by my sixth-grade teacher, who one day made me sit under the blackboard with my face to the wall while she told the rest of the class how and why she disliked me. Another incident had occurred only a few months beforehand when I had a mental block while being interviewed and filmed in a television studio.

God also revealed to me an image of myself as a target: I was surrounded by people, and they were firing arrows right at me and in me. I realized that because of my past experiences I would subconsciously brace myself for a similar onslaught every time I walked into a classroom or a public speaking setting. I was waiting and expecting to fail and to be humiliated. This was what was causing me to be nervous, resulting in my voice being strained. God gave me this scripture, which I was to hold on to as a promise and as a weapon against any future onslaught that would threaten my confidence.

I sought the LORD, and he answered me; he delivered me from all my fears. Those who look to him are radiant; their faces are never covered with shame.

—PSALM 34:4–5

What a beautiful new image! What a stunning promise! Never again would I have to stand up scared with the prospect of shame being shot at me. Freedom from shame meant no more fear of embarrassment, humiliation, or failure. Instead, I could stand with my face radiant, reflecting an inner peace and joy, the beautiful fruit of a heart delivered from fear.

I have come to realize that many apparent fears are symptoms of deeper fears. To properly address the surface fear you have to dig deeper. Ask yourself the question, What am I really afraid of? Deeper fears often reflect issues of rejection, abandonment, and disapproval. I know God can reveal to you what these fears are and then give you the power to overcome them. To do this, you must arm yourself with a scripture that speaks to your heart about your situation. Memorize and meditate upon this word. Over time your mind will be transformed, your spirit strengthened, and your faith built. With the delivering grace of Jesus and the power of God's Word you can walk out of fear and into freedom.

3. Fear of Success

Successful is the term commonly attributed to someone who has attained fame, wealth, or power due to an impressive achievement. Success gives us a voice and a platform with which to impact and influence others. Fear of success, therefore, is actually the fear of doing well in life—of accomplishing feats; becoming prosperous; being influential; or having favor, honor, and recognition. This fear can result in a person settling for less than their worth or aspiring to less than what they are capable of achieving.

I believe women need to boldly and uncompromisingly address these fears. Women who make the decision to rise will be women who have chosen to be influential and powerful, accomplished and successful. Let these words of Marianne Williamson inspire you.

Our Deepest Fear

Our deepest fear is not that we are inadequate. Our deepest fear is that we are powerful beyond measure. It is our light, not our darkness that most frightens us. We ask ourselves, Who am I to be brilliant, gorgeous, talented, fabulous? Actually, who are you not to be? You are a child of God. Your playing small does not serve the world. There's nothing enlightened about shrinking so that other people won't feel insecure around you. We are all meant to shine, as children do. We were born to make manifest the glory of God that is within us. It's not just in some of us; it's in everyone. And as we let our own light shine, we unconsciously give other people permission to do the same. As we're liberated from our own fear, our presence automatically liberates others.[2]

To rise as women and become people of influence, we need to see ourselves through God's eyes. That we are:

Big

Bold

Bright

Beautiful

As children of the most High God, we are extraordinary beings. We are talented, gorgeous, and powerful women. We can accomplish our most amazing aspirations. We are worthy and deserving of success. We can impact and influence the lives of others. And we're born to display the glory of God—not just some of us, but all of us!

What does this mean for you and me? No longer can we allow ourselves to under-achieve due to poor self-esteem or false humility. We have to learn personal disciplines to overcome fear, pessimistic thoughts, or waning motivation. It's time for each one of us to take charge of our lives and overcome the obstacles that may hold us back from reaching our potential and shining our light.

There are many aspects to success that can cause us to shrink back and respond in fear. Some of these factors are rarely acknowledged, but they are very important to address. Success will bring favor, recognition, influence, and wealth. These rewards of success can result in their own set of challenges. Success commonly will also set you apart and move you ahead of your peers. It will probably change the dynamic of relationships. True friendships will survive your success; other relationships may not. All these factors can be disconcerting and provide compelling reasons for not pursuing success in all its fullness.

A wise woman will recognize and be prepared for what success may do in all aspects of her world. As a lost and insecure teenager, I told God, "I don't want to be beneath the crowd. I don't want to be above the crowd. I just want to be one of the crowd." In my late thirties, I was reminded about this, and I sensed God saying to me, "Amanda, I have not called you to be one of the crowd. I have called you to be above the crowd." I realized that to make the choice to rise, I had to be prepared to be different and to stand out. So will you.

4. The One and Only Fear

I have stated on a number of occasions throughout this chapter that *all* fears may be overcome. However, I'm going to contradict myself and say that there is actually one fear that must remain with us forever. It is the fear of God. To fear God does not mean that we need to be scared or frightened of God. It means having a deep reverential awe of His might and His majesty.

When you fear God, He is your Lord. That means you not only believe in Jesus, but you are also obedient and submitted to His authority in your life. When you truly fear God you are able to walk with the assurance that no challenge, trial, attack, or unforeseen circumstance can do you harm. You can rest knowing that He is guiding and protecting you all the days of your life. You can be like the Proverbs 31 woman, who "can laugh at the days to come" (Prov. 31:25). When we fear God we do not fear.

But blessed is the man who trusts in the LORD, whose confidence is in him. He will be like a tree planted by the water that sends out its roots by the stream. It does not fear when heat comes; its leaves are always green. It has no worries in a year of drought and never fails to bear fruit.

—JEREMIAH 17:7–8

The angel of the LORD encamps around those who fear him, and he delivers them. . . . Fear the LORD, you his saints, for those who fear him lack nothing. . . . A righteous man may have many troubles, but the LORD delivers him from them all.

—PSALM 34:7, 9, 19

HOW TO OVERCOME FEAR

Fear is a natural part of being engaged in life. In some ways we must accept that at times various fears will rise in our hearts. However we must not ignore or become complacent about them. It is up to us to contend with our fears. Our first battle as soldiers in God's army is to fight against our personal enemy: our own fears. As women who are growing and rising, we are not to give way to fear. We must face fear and push through it. We cannot let fear shackle and imprison us. We cannot allow fear to steal our joy, dim our lights, squash our potential, and hinder our influence. We must rise to overcome our fears. Let's look at how we can do this.

Understand That You Are Not Alone

The emotional and physical responses that fear produces may leave you feeling isolated and defenseless. It's so helpful to know that these are only feelings, not the truth. God is with you, and He can help you. You do not have to face fear alone and without a weapon. He is right there to encourage and enable you with His presence and His power.

For two years of my life I lived in Cebu City in the Philippines. Before I moved there I went on a reconnaissance trip to see the land that was going to become my new home. I was traveling back to Australia on my own, and because of the airplane flights I had to stop over for a couple of days in the capital city, Manila. I remember feeling very scared and alone. I was fearful of an unknown culture, frightened I would get lost in a big city, and worried the taxi drivers would take advantage of me. In the midst of my fear, God gave me this scripture from Isaiah 41:13: "For I am the LORD, your God, who takes hold of your right hand and says to you, Do not fear; I will help you." I still remember walking around the busy streets of Manila conscious of God holding my right hand. He was with me—leading me, guiding me, and protecting me.

Here are some further passages of scripture that highlight the closeness of God in the midst of fear.

> I took you from the ends of the earth, from its farthest corners I called you. I said, "You are my servant"; I have chosen you and have not rejected you. So do not fear, for I am with you; do not be dismayed, for I am your God. I will strengthen you and help you; I will uphold you with my righteous right hand.
>
> —ISAIAH 41:9–10

> Fear not, for I have redeemed you; I have summoned you by name; you are mine. When you pass through the waters, I will be with you; and when you pass through the rivers, they will not sweep over you. When you walk through the fire, you will not be burned; the flames will not set you ablaze.
>
> —ISAIAH 43:1–2

You have already heard part of my story about my fears of public speaking, but I want to share something more with you.

I was in my final year at university when I had a major public speaking meltdown. One day in class we were asked to conduct a debate. I had never been in a debate before, and we were given only thirty minutes to prepare. I have come to realize I don't enjoy speaking off the cuff; I gain confidence in having time to prepare what I'm going to say. So in this situation I was very uncomfortable, to say the least.

When it was my turn to respond, I walked out to the front of the classroom, and I opened my mouth to speak. To my horror, no sound came out. It was as if someone had put a vice around my throat. I felt a hot flush of embarrassment rise up my neck and cover my face. Then, in front of the whole class, I burst into tears and ran out of the classroom all the way home. Once there, I sobbed and sobbed in humiliation and frustration. I felt embarrassed, useless, and defeated.

In the midst of this vulnerable state, I had to present my final major research report to all my fellow students and a number of my lecturers only one week later. I was so afraid. All I could do was pray and trust that God would be my help. I held onto one scripture:

> *Such confidence as this is ours through Christ before God. Not that we are competent in ourselves to claim anything for ourselves, but our competence comes from God.*
>
> —2 CORINTHIANS 3:4–5

I vividly remember standing up that day to address my class and my teachers. I felt supernaturally strong. I was clothed in a confidence that I could only attribute to God. I felt His presence with me. I did a great presentation. I actually topped the class. From this experience I discovered that in my weakness, God can make me strong. I also learned that I never have to face fear on my own; He will be with me and He will empower me. All I have to do is ask Him and trust Him.

Through these events which have happened in my life I know that:

God is with me.

However, I have also discovered something that is just as important:

God is in me.

As Christians we need to be reminded that when we are filled with the Holy Spirit we actually carry the presence and power of God. The Bible says the same spirit which raised Jesus from the dead also lives inside us (Rom. 8:11). The Holy Spirit is what empowers believers to be bright and bold. When the disciples were filled with the Holy Spirit, they preached and saw thousands saved, they prophesied and spoke the words of God, they laid hands on the sick and saw many healed, and they prayed and saw the dead raised to life.

For God did not give us a spirit of timidity, but a spirit of power, of love and of self-discipline.

—2 Timothy 1:7

Stop, Stand, Step

"But my righteous one will live by faith. And if he shrinks back, I will not be pleased with him." But we are not of those who shrink back and are destroyed, but of those who believe and are saved.

—Hebrews 10:38–39

The "fight or flight" response was only given a name in the 1920s; however, we see it so vividly described here in the scriptures. When confronted with a fearful situation our reaction is often to shrink back. I am sure we can all relate to these synonyms for the word *shrink*: *dwindle, decrease, decline, diminish,* and *disappear.*

When I am in a situation that confronts me, I often feel myself stepping backwards. I want to retreat and run, withdraw and hide. In my heart, I can feel small, scared, and powerless. If I do act on these impulses, the Scriptures say that God is not pleased with me. Why? Because He understands that in giving way to fear I have allowed it to conquer me. When we allow fear to master or dominate us, that area of our world has become spoiled, damaged, and defeated.

Hebrews 10:38–39 is giving us a mandate from God: You are not one who shrinks back! Don't you love that? I suggest you learn these words by heart so that when fear rises, so does the Word of God. The battle over fear begins in your heart. The Word must become louder than any intimidation and carry more power than any fear. Say over and over and over again, "I am not one who shrinks back and is destroyed, but one who stands my ground and moves forward."

When faced with a fearful situation, the first thing to do—despite everything inside you screaming, "Run"—is to stop retreating and to stand your ground. By doing this you are taking a stance that declares, "I am getting ready to confront!" At this point you can allow yourself to feel the fear, identify its source, and acknowledge the physical symptoms that have been produced in your body. This process helps to disengage the power they have over you. Calm yourself by taking a few deep breaths and build your faith by boldly repeating a scripture you have memorized.

Next, take the first step forward into fear's territory by actually doing the thing that you fear. You speak, you sing, you dance, you act, you climb, you paint, you swim, you drive, you pick up the phone, you introduce yourself, you travel alone, you ask for the promotion, you start a business—you do whatever it is that is triggering your fear. You will discover that as you continue to confront the fear, it will eventually be conquered.

Put on Courage

Fear and faith are polar opposites. To move from fear to faith, we have to "put on" courage. Courage is a choice. It is the decision to bravely face a difficult or dangerous situation despite fear. I am not a naturally outgoing, bold, and courageous girl. So, fear has surrounded almost everything I have ever attempted or initiated in my life. I have had to learn and am still learning to overcome fear. I appreciate the truth in these quotations:

> *Anything I've ever done that ultimately was worthwhile initially scared me to death.*
>
> —BETTY BENDER[2]

> *Whenever we take a chance and enter unfamiliar territory or put ourselves into the world in a new way, we experience fear. Very often this fear keeps us from moving ahead with our lives. The trick is to feel the fear and do it anyway. So many of us short-circuit our living, by choosing the path that is most comfortable. Realize that fear will never go away as long as you continue to grow. The only way to get rid of the fear of doing something is to go out and do it.*
>
> —SUSAN JEFFERS[3]

God provides opportunities in everyday life for us to grow in boldness and courage. It may be through playing a sport, taking up a new hobby, or embarking on a different career. As a teenager I loved the game of softball, and in my thirties I took it up again. During my school years, I was always a B-grade player and had never scored a home run. But I returned to softball a different Amanda, an Amanda who possessed courage that I had lacked as a teenager.

Every time I walked up to the home plate, I firmly took my place, eyed the pitcher, and said to myself, "Amanda, you are going to whack this ball!" I learned that I could put the "grunt" that was now in my spirit behind my bat and onto the ball. I was proud of myself that year. I scored the most home runs in our team and received the home run trophy for the season. A few years later I was able to coach my daughter's softball team, and I taught those nine year olds how to have a "girly grunt." They loved this concept. They would call out to each other when they would get up to bat: "Come on; don't forget the 'girly grunt.'" I have since stopped playing softball, but there have been many occasions when I have applied this same boldness, courage, and "girly grunt" to other areas of my life.

Humans have a need for both security and risk. As individuals we are more likely to favor one than the other. I find it interesting that the same situation that causes fear in one person can actually bring excitement to another. What some perceive as a threat, others perceive as a thrill. I believe that to overcome fear, we need to push through our need for security and discover the risk-taking side of our personality. Psychologists say, "If a child has not had a serious fall within the first year of life, they are being too closely guarded."[5] We need to apply this truth to our own adult lives. We cannot guard ourselves too closely or live with too much caution. I agree with this sentiment by the French philosopher Simone Weil: "The boredom produced by a complete absence of risk is also sickness of the soul."[6]

Let me conclude this chapter with an inspirational quotation that challenges us to overcome fear and make wise choices by putting on courage.

Whenever we are struck by fear, we are standing at a fork in the road. One branch of the road leads to cowardice, the other to courage. One fork leads to our desires and dreams, the other to disappointment and despair.

—CHUCK GALLOZI[7]

Let's make the choice to be women who will turn aside from cowardly ways and take the road of courage. This road will take us on a wonderful journey, experiencing the fulfillment of our potential and purpose and the satisfaction of a successful life. We must always remember that fear breeds failure, but courage produces confidence, and when confidence multiplies, extraordinary lives are created.

Time to Reflect

Take a moment to:

- Identify what role fear plays in your life. How does it make you feel? How has it kept you small, stuck, hiding, or lacking in confidence?
- Identify the fears you have. What conditions, activities, objects, animals, people, places, or situations do you fear? What are your deep inner fears?
- Identify a number of events in your life where you have experienced the "fight or flight" response. What were your physical and emotional responses?
- Identify some occasions when you have overcome fear. What did you think and do to confront and conquer this fear? How did you put on courage?

Time to Act

- Identify one fear that you commonly face and would like to overcome. Write down what this fear is and then dig deeper by asking yourself, What do I really fear?
- Find a scripture that will build your faith in this area and begin to memorize and meditate on it.
- Write down some practical steps that you need to implement to overcome this fear. If possible, make a date in your diary when you will confront this fear.

Chapter Eight

SATAN'S SHACKLES

Finally, be strong in the Lord and in his mighty power. Put on the full armor of God so that you can take your stand against the devil's schemes. For our struggle is not against flesh and blood, but against the rulers, against the authorities, against the powers of this dark world and against the spiritual forces of evil in the heavenly realms.

—EPHESIANS 6:10–12

I firmly believe that the devil doesn't like women. He has tried to stop us and keep us shackled for a long, long time. To do this, he has devised many varied schemes using different people, religions, governments, laws, and customs. He has infiltrated cultures with lies and false beliefs. He has limited education and career opportunities and even provoked the misinterpretation of some scriptures. For centuries, Satan has kept women in physical, social, and spiritual bondage, locked up and locked away. He has tried to dim or even extinguish the influence of women by keeping their lights "under a bowl." His goal has always been to keep women feeling small and insignificant. But I believe a new day has come. Justice and truth are rising, and women are being set free.

Throughout my life there have been a number of occasions when I have felt a burden deep within my spirit regarding women and the lack of recognition and release they have experienced, particularly within the church environment. On one of these occasions, when I was in prayer, I had a vision that changed my life and the message of which will stay with me forever.

I saw two demonic spirits, each one with a specific assignment. The first spirit was to keep women imprisoned and prevent them from being released; symbolically it was represented by a chain and shackle around a woman's ankle. I saw the shackle being broken and the woman walking free. As for the second spirit, I'll tell you more about that in the next chapter. For now, we are going to explore the significance of this first spirit and Satan's shackles.

WHAT ARE THESE SHACKLES?

This vision very strongly conveyed to me that Satan has assigned demons to keep women subjugated. It's interesting to note that the woman in my vision was not in jail. Rather, she was imprisoned with shackles around her ankles. This says to me that the devil doesn't like women moving and is threatened by the thought of us advancing, so he has focused his energies on keeping our legs and our feet chained. He has allowed us restricted movement but hinders us from walking or running with complete freedom. I see this spirit and these shackles represent two things:

1. Demonic lies regarding the value, status, and roles of women. These lies have infiltrated the hearts and minds of people and cultures. This has caused them to live with false mind-sets, beliefs, and attitudes and in a state of deception or ignorance.
2. People who have not allowed women to rise and fulfill their potential and purpose.

THE STATUS OF WOMEN WORLDWIDE

In a society where the rights and potential of women are constrained, no man can be truly free. He may have power, but he will not have freedom.

—MARY ROBINSON, PRESIDENT OF IRELAND[1]

History has shown that in many nations across the world women have been and are still being suppressed and oppressed. The last United Nations World Conference on Women was held in Beijing, China, in 1995. The aim of this conference was to advance and empower women. This worldwide body of delegates concluded that:

Deeply entrenched attitudes and practices perpetuate inequality and discrimination against women, in public and private life, in all parts of the world. Accordingly, implementation requires change in values, attitudes, practices and priorities at all levels.[2]

Some of the attitudes and practices that are embedded in the fabric of many societies that demoralize, exploit, and restrict women include:

- the attitude that men are superior to women and that they have the right to rule over women;
- the attitude that women should not hold positions of leadership, share power, or contribute to decision making;
- practices that reflect inequalities and inadequacies in healthcare, education, training, employment, access to resources, and opportunities for advancement;
- laws that give women few or no legal rights because they are regarded as the property of their fathers or husbands;
- practices such as female circumcision, forced marriages, domestic violence, sexual exploitation, human trafficking, and female infanticide.

OUR BELIEFS AND MIND-SETS

We have all been raised under a multitude of influences. These have shaped how we view the value, status, and roles of women. Some of these influences have been positive and some of them negative. The beliefs we hold are very potent because they are deeply embedded in our subconscious. We are often not aware of these mind-sets or the effect they have on our thinking and behavior.

If you have been nurtured and educated in a family, church, society, or country that was prejudiced against women, then some of the beliefs you hold may not reflect God's view of women. Such views can be so subconscious that even women may discriminate against themselves. Much of this misguided thinking and behavior was taught or modeled to us when we were little girls. Some of the influences that have impacted our lives are:

- parental values and behaviors;
- cultural traditions and heritage;
- country of birth;

- religious practices and beliefs;
- education systems; and
- the media, advertising, and propaganda.

Changing Times: In Cultures, Communities, Countries

Over the last century, particularly the last fifty years, there have been dramatic changes for women in many countries and cultures around the world. There has been a progression in rights, roles, and opportunities for women. Significant social changes have also occurred that have resulted in women gaining greater freedom and expression. The most noteworthy of these changes have been:

- better education,
- broader career choices,
- increased pay for women,
- positions in government and business,
- technological and medical advancements,
- invention of the contraceptive pill,
- women working outside the home,
- introduction of childcare,
- women marrying older and having fewer babies, and
- increased accessibility to divorce.

Most of these advances reflect positive progress; however, it is interesting and necessary to note that these changes have also resulted in some negative consequences and challenges for women. An article titled "We've Come a Long Way, Baby" that was printed in a popular Australian magazine, *The Australian Women's Weekly*, makes this poignant remark: "There is no doubt that better education and women working outside the home were two of the most significant social changes of the 20th century, but whether women are happy with their lot is questionable. Many women battle with the problem of daily fatigue, as they try to combine a paid job with looking after their home and family."[3] Greater opportunities and increased liberties don't necessarily bring true freedom. The great struggle for most women is to find a balance between managing a home, raising a family, and pursuing a career.

The last half-century has also brought a shift in attitude. Years ago I was given a copy of an article titled "The Good Wife's Guide," supposedly from the May 1955 edition of *Housekeeping Monthly* magazine. This article gave wives some tips about how to prepare for a husband's arrival home from work. Some of these tips are wise, as it is important for wives to respect, care, and serve their husbands in practical ways. However, there are under- lying attitudes in this article that imply men are more important than women and that a wife's opinion and needs are secondary to that of her husband. I believe that a wife should serve her husband out of love and respect, not from a position of subservience or inferiority. The following points are extracts from this article, which highlight these "old" attitudes.

- Listen to him. You may have a dozen important things to tell him, but the moment of his arrival is not the time. Let him talk first—remember his topics of conversation are more important than yours.

- Make the evening his. Never complain if he comes home late or goes out to dinner or other places of entertainment without you. Instead try to understand his world of strain and pressure and his very real need to be at home and relax.

- Don't complain if he's late home for dinner or even if he stays out all night. Count this as minor, compared to what he might have gone through that day.

- Don't ask him questions about his actions or question his judgment or integrity. Remember he is the master of the house and as such will always exercise his will with fairness and truthfulness. You have no right to question him.[4]

Some of you reading this chapter will be able to relate to this "old" world. A younger reader is probably experiencing a mix of disbelief and amusement. Obviously much has changed in the last fifty years.

These days, in most western marriages men and women are more like partners, working as a team to raise the children, conduct the household chores,
and support one another's personal and career goals. However, in many
families and societies the old attitudes, mind-sets, and beliefs still keep the
shackles around women's legs.

CHANGING TIMES: IN THE CHURCH

I believe that more has been done to break these shackles in secular society
(especially western society) than within some areas of the church. In many
denominations there is still heated debate about female ordination and
about whether women are allowed to preach, teach, pastor, plant churches,
lead, or function as elders on church boards. In many churches, the roles
and opportunities for women are still limited and stereotyped.

Women have traditionally served in roles of hospitality, caring for children,
intercessory prayer, and perhaps administration. I find it ironic that many
of the famous missionaries throughout history were women. Church elders
wouldn't allow these women to lead or preach in their local churches. But,
they would willingly send them to the other side of the globe to convert
the "heathens" and plant churches in remote, "uncivilized," and often
dangerous places.

Within the church environment, some men find it difficult to release women
into positions of leadership or to sit under the ministry of women. I recall
one of Cindy Jacobs's stories: When she preached, all the men responded by
standing up, turning their chairs around, and sitting with their backs to her.
I have had some similar experiences. I was in the middle of preaching one
day when a man suddenly yelled out, "What would you know? You're only a
woman." In moments like these, it's essential that a woman is convinced she
has been called and anointed by God to minister from the pulpit!

Most of my life I have attended church, and throughout this time I have seen
significant changes and advancements in what women are permitted to do
and the positions they can hold. I believe the teachings found in Kenneth
Hagin's book *The Woman Question* and Cindy Jacobs's *Women of Destiny*
have been instrumental in revolutionizing the thinking patterns concerning
this issue. In many churches we are now seeing women ordained, preaching

from the pulpit, teaching in Bible colleges, and holding positions of leadership. The tide is definitely turning, but it has not yet fully turned. There are still denominations that refuse to embrace change and female church members who are frustrated at the lack of opportunities to express the gifts and call in their lives.

The term *established culture* refers to the customs and behaviors of people living in a community, which they perform without conscious thought. Many churches don't yet have an established culture of empowering women because the issue is still being discussed. I am of the opinion we need to stop talking and start releasing! When this happens, over time, a new culture will be established.

OTHER PEOPLE WHO HINDER

The shackles around our ankles may also represent people who hold us back or lock us away. Our relationships have the potential to empower or to imprison us. These relationships include interaction with our parents, our spouse, our children, our bosses, our leaders, our pastors, our friends, and, yes, even ourselves. Women sometimes place themselves in relationships that keep them small, hidden, and intimidated.

In my roles as a pastor and life coach, I have met women who have been hindered by the attitudes and actions of their husbands. Some husbands have been well-meaning but misguided in their overly protective ways, keeping their wives hiding behind them. In other marriages, the wives have not been included in the making of decisions or are kept in the dark about important matters. I've seen this happen most often in the area of household finances. This lack of mutual involvement divides the marriage and disempowers the wife. In other instances, I have met women who have dreams they want to pursue, but their partners are unsupportive or even prohibitive.

Unfortunately, even women are responsible for restraining and hindering other women. Insecurities, jealousy, and pride can result in some women holding tightly onto positions when others are crying out to be raised and released. Women of all ages and levels of maturity need to look out for other women to mentor. It is such a powerful thing to validate and encourage another woman and provide opportunities that will enable her to grow and blossom. It is important that we are women who choose to do this for other women.

SHACKLES BROKEN

Satan has spent centuries belittling women and weaving a web of lies into a formidable worldwide network of oppression to hold them down ... He cannot afford to have women walking upright. He desperately needs to keep them down. But Satan cannot do this forever.
—ED SILVOSO, *WOMEN: GOD'S SECRET WEAPON*[5]

How wonderful is this statement: "But Satan cannot do this forever"? In my vision, the chain and shackle around the woman's ankle does break, and it does fall off. I sense that God smiles every time a shackle is removed and a woman is released. His heart is delighted because when a shackle is broken, an individual woman is able to move forward and become all that God has created her to be. When this happens, justice has triumphed and Satan has been defeated.

In your majesty ride forth victoriously in behalf of truth, humility and righteousness; let your right hand display awesome deeds. Let your sharp arrows pierce the hearts of the king's enemies; let the nations fall beneath your feet. Your throne, O God, will last for ever and ever; a scepter of justice will be the scepter of your kingdom.
—PSALM 45:4–6

How, then, do these shackles get broken? I believe we need a multifaceted strategy to destroy them. Let's look at five different tactics.

Tactic 1: Prayer

For our struggle is not against flesh and blood, but against the rulers, against the authorities, against the powers of this dark world and against the spiritual forces of evil in the heavenly realms.
—EPHESIANS 6:12

For though we live in the world, we do not wage war as the world does. The weapons we fight with are not the weapons of the world. On the contrary, they have divine power to demolish strongholds.

—2 CORINTHIANS 10:3–4

These scriptures put this issue into perspective: it is spiritual in origin. Yes, there may be specific people, organizations, and even governments that want to suppress and oppress women; but the root of the problem is Satan, his demons, his dark world, and his evil ways. We cannot address this issue with any other strategies until we first fight it in prayer. Our number one weapon is prayer. We must bind the devil's power. We must pray against deception. We must pray against false mindsets. We must pray for truth to be revealed. We must pray for hearts to be changed. We must pray for women to be released. Put simply, we must *pray*!

Tactic 2: Teaching Truth

For centuries the devil has perpetrated lies in communities and churches. Unfortunately, the source of many of these lies has come from the misinterpretation of the Bible. These lies have kept people ignorant and deceived about God's true view of women.

Therefore, it is of the utmost importance that biblical truth is accurately and fearlessly taught in our churches, small groups, and Bible colleges. These demonic shackles will only be broken when the truth of the Word of God is revealed and then applied. I have discovered that ignorance is never bliss. When people are unaware of the truth, they often make decisions and take actions that are based on false information or presumptions. Chapter 11 of this book is entitled "Truth Revealed." In it I address some of the incorrect teaching and misunderstanding that abounds throughout Christendom regarding the value, status, and roles of women. The church should be leading the way in championing and empowering women.

Tactic 3: Discipleship

Probably the most effective way to liberate men and women in the church is through discipleship. In a community or business setting this is referred to as mentoring. Both discipleship and mentoring create an enriching two-way relationship. The disciple-maker or mentor acts as a model to emulate, a teacher to learn from, and a guide to give advice. The most powerful part of the relationship is the more mature, experienced person believing in and encouraging the less experienced disciple, causing them to grow and to rise. You cannot place a value on this relationship. It is priceless because it can change a person's life forever.

There are three crucial aspects to successful disciple-making:

- Recognize the potential talent, skill, character, and calling in a person.
- Raise the person by encouraging, training, and correcting them and providing opportunities that will promote their growth and development.
- Release them into positions in which they can use their gifts and fulfill their God-given call.

If women are going to be released in our churches, they need to be discipled by both men and women. I don't know anyone who doesn't long to be believed in and mentored. We all need spiritual moms and dads. In the churches that I visit, many women tell me they are looking for mentors. My simple answer to them is: If you can't find one, be one.

Tactic 4: Repentance, Restoration, and Reconciliation

Many years ago I heard Cindy Jacobs teach at a conference. She spoke on the necessity to breach the gender gap and restore male and female relationships. In this meeting she allowed time for a number of men to publicly apologize to women for their false beliefs, bad attitudes, and wrong behaviors. She then asked all the men to pray for the women present in that meeting. I personally found this experience very powerful and significant.

Pastor Ed Silvoso says:

> Lack of reconciliation between men and women is what keeps in place the worldwide system of lies the devil uses to dishonor women and to cripple men... The need for wholeness between genders goes beyond male and female. It affects institutions, secular and religious, as well as families... Reconciliation between men and women is the key. But within this key there is another one: the restoration of women.[6]

For women to be restored and released, the reconciliation of men and women is vital. What is needed is repentance and forgiveness. These are the keys which will open the shackle locks. I have personally found that if men do not love, value, and respect their mothers, wives, and daughters, then they will not respect other women. Repentance, restoration, and reconciliation must therefore begin in our homes and our closest relationships.

Tactic 5: Strategies, Policies, and Laws

The final stage in promoting the worldwide advancement and empowerment of women is to establish favorable strategies, policies, and laws. For example, the platform for action that was established at the United Nations Fourth World Conference for Women, which I cited earlier in this chapter, called upon governments, institutions, and organizations at community, national, and international levels to publicly make time-specific goals to improve the status of women. Large, worldwide public and private institutions such as the World Bank and World Trade Organization made commitments to financially assist the implementation of programs that would benefit women in such areas as health, education, decision making, business, and legal reforms.

I was saddened, however, by a report compiled by the Advisory Committee on Equal Opportunities of Women and Men that was presented to the Parliamentary Assembly at the Council of Europe in April 2004. It said:

> *Unfortunately, the reality of the situation of women in the world today is depressing and in some areas even worse than in 1995. The backlash against women's rights and gender equality has taken many forms. Few governments have lived up to their commitments made in Beijing—there has not only been a lack of implementation of the Platform for Action but also a lack of political will to change the status quo.*[7]

I believe the reason for this complacency, lack of action, and further subjugation of women is simply because this is a spiritual issue. Parliaments, policies, and programs are valuable. However, if the root cause is Satan, their effectiveness will be minimal. Therefore, we must first pray and fight this battle in the heavenlies.

SHACKLES ON MY ANKLES!

We need to address one further question: How do I respond if I'm in a situation where I feel shackled? I believe there are a number of things you can do. If the situation or relationship is one in which it would be inappropriate to remove yourself, then you need to trust God and pray. Only God can give you the peace and grace to walk through these challenges, and only God can provide a way when it looks impossible. For women who are in destructive relationships, it is important for you to establish strong boundaries or even to cut ties.

In some relationships and on some occasions, it may be appropriate for you to speak up and speak out. I know that God has sometimes told me to be quiet and at other times to speak what is on my mind and in my heart. Some women need to find their voice. But when we do speak, we must do it with wisdom and respect. God does not want us to be contentious or rebellious women, but rather women who are pure and humble yet filled with strength and conviction. I believe we can apply the wisdom of Martin Luther King Jr. from the words he spoke in his famous "I Have a Dream" speech, which called for racial equality in America.

> *But there is something that I must say to my people who stand on the warm threshold which leads into the palace of justice: In the process of gaining our rightful place, we must not be guilty of wrongful deeds. Let us not seek to satisfy our thirst for freedom by drinking from the cup of bitterness and hatred. We must forever conduct our struggle on the high plane of dignity and discipline.*
>
> —MARTIN LUTHER KING[8]

As I have already said, there have been times in my life when I have felt deeply burdened by the limitations that have been placed around women. My heart has cried out to God for women to be given opportunities and positions to fully express the call of God that burns deep inside their hearts. Perhaps you, too, have felt a similar burden.

But in the quest to see women rise, we must not fly our feminist flags. We must not fight for power or position or the need to rule or reign. We do not need to compete with others, but rather we must work with men and other women in complementary and cooperative partnerships, both in the church and in society. Our only fight must be against Satan, the one who detests us because he is afraid of us.

So what is my dream and—dare I say it—God's dream?

- Women who have a particular calling, gifting, and the character required for different positions in the church will not be overlooked or kept restricted because of their gender.
- Women will be allowed to have a voice in places that have long been dominated by men, such as preaching and teaching roles and positions of governmental authority.
- Women will be developed, discipled, trained, and released into these positions.
- Christian women will rise to positions where they are leading and influencing others in the society in which they live.
- Women all around the world will be set free from physical, social, and spiritual bondage.

I love the words in the song "Shackles (Praise You)" by Mary Mary. Let me change the lyrics a little so that they express my vision: "Take the shackles off our feet so we can rise. We want to serve Him; we want to serve Him."

TIME TO REFLECT

- Identify the positive and negative influences that have affected the way you view the value, status, and roles of women.
  Your parents' values and behaviors.
  Your cultural traditions and heritage.
  The country in which you live and/or were raised.
  Your religious practices and beliefs.
  The education system within which you were schooled.
  The media, advertising, and propaganda around you.
- Identify examples in which women's feet are shackled. Apply this question to yourself, your family, your friends, your community, your country, and internationally.
- Identify changes that have taken place in the last fifty years for women in your country, community, and church. Consider if these changes have been positive or negative.

TIME TO ACT

- Identify a couple of women you can encourage and mentor. Make a list of some practical ways you can effectively disciple them.
- Spend time praying against the demonic strongholds behind the shackles you have identified.

Chapter Nine

DEMONIC OPPOSITION

In the previous chapter I shared with you a vision that God showed me of two spirits that are appointed by the devil specifically to hinder and restrain women. The first spirit was represented as a chain and shackle around the woman's ankle and was described in the preceding chapter.

It is time now to tell you about the second spirit I saw in my vision. Many of you will have experienced the effects of this spirit's power but have likely been ignorant of what it was you were facing or how to overcome it.

In my vision, this demonic spirit was very dark, very big, and very oppressive. It positioned itself right in front of the woman, who had now been released from her shackles and was walking forward in her newfound freedom. The assigned task of this spirit was to thwart the woman's attempts to advance and to rise. It stationed itself like a huge brick wall directly in the path of the woman so that she couldn't climb over it, walk around it, or pull it down. I heard the words, "Once the shackles have been broken and others have released her, the woman will confront a demon that will try and stop her." The words continued, "It is only the woman herself who can push through this spirit. Only then will she be able to move forward to victory."

I had a very strong impression that the woman felt alone, small, and scared. No one was able or permitted to help her fight this spirit. She was the only one who had the right and the authority to overcome it. She could not walk around it or over it but had to find a way to walk through its presence and force. After the woman boldly and bravely confronted this spirit, she was easily taken through the "wall" to the other side. The spirit was now behind her, and the woman was free to continue walking along her journey.

I clearly saw that this spirit deliberately positioned itself directly in front of the woman, attempting to prevent her from progressing forward. I am convinced that any woman who makes the choice to rise and further the kingdom of God will encounter this demonic spirit. Before any advancement or promotion is possible, this spirit will try and stop you and knock you off your tracks.

When God shows me a vision, I ask Him lots of questions. On this occasion I asked Him to help me understand this demonic spirit. I wanted to know what it looked like, how it behaved, and how it could be defeated. What God impressed upon me was that this spirit was the same one that resided in the giant Goliath. I proceeded to do a Bible study on Goliath and the battle he fought with David. I'm going to share with you what I discovered about this demonic spirit and what I have personally experienced. But first, I suggest you pause for a moment and read the story in your own Bible. You'll find it in 1 Samuel 17.

THE STORY OF GOLIATH AND DAVID

Let me begin by giving you some historical background to this story. In Old Testament times when two nations were at war they would sometimes decide not to fight with their whole army in one big, bloody battle. Rather, each side would select their best warrior, and the two of them would battle it out until one was dead. The warrior who was still alive at the end brought victory to the army and the nation he represented.

In this story, Israel, God's chosen nation, was fighting against the nation of Philistia. The armies had set up camp on hills opposite each other, and they were separated by a valley. The Philistine army had chosen a giant, Goliath, to be their warrior envoy. The Israelite nation had no representative. Not a single soldier in the entire army felt confident to fight Goliath.

In this campaign, every morning and every evening, thousands of soldiers prepared for battle. The armies positioned themselves in two parallel lines and as they faced each other they shouted their battle cries. Goliath would then step forward and boldly send out a challenge for someone from the Israelite army to be his contender. No one from the nation of Israel answered his challenge. This happened twice a day for forty days. Fear, terror, and intimidation infiltrated and immobilized the entire Hebrew army.

It was not until a young man, by the name of David, arrived at the army camp to bring supplies to his older brothers, that the situation started to shift. David arose and chose to be Goliath's contender. Filled with faith and a holy passion, he fought and killed the giant and brought victory to the nation of Israel.

The Goliath Spirit: What Is It Like?

As I studied this story, the first thing I noticed was that Goliath was called a champion. This meant he was a skilled fighter and a seasoned warrior who had fought many battles and scored many wins. He was a warrior filled with an insatiable hunger and a brazen confidence to fight and kill every opponent. As a champion he had never been defeated. He was a hero to his nation: the one who held the trophy and the title. The second thing I noticed was that Goliath was BIG: a giant towering over the Israelites at nine feet tall. He was clothed with powerful armor that made him appear even more impressive and oppressive.

From these observations, I realized that the spirit we are dealing with is big, strong, and forceful. It is ready, willing, and able to contend and compete with you and me. This demonic spirit is well acquainted with the art of war and the skill and thrill of fighting. It is a veteran; it has been playing this game of terrorizing men and women for a long time, attempting to overshadow us and overpower us, making us feel small and insignificant.

His Motivation: Defiance

> *Goliath, the Philistine champion from Gath, stepped out from his lines and shouted his usual defiance.... Then the Philistine said, "This day I defy the ranks of Israel! Give me a man and let us fight each other."*
> —1 Samuel 17:23, 10

Every morning and evening for forty days, Goliath declared these words, which expressed his inner compulsion to fight this battle. He was consumed with an insidious, passionate fire that fueled his hatred and his zeal to fight. Goliath was filled with a defiant spirit. He was no doubt aware that by defying the nation of Israel, he was actually defying God.

To *defy* means "to contend, challenge and confront." This is exactly what Goliath did to the Israelite army and what this spirit aims to do to you. It will stand up and block your way. It will try to hinder you with seemingly insurmountable obstacles. It will not only challenge you to combat but also contest and belittle your authority and your ability.

Today this same spirit that was in Goliath will do anything to defy God, the people of God, and the purposes of God. It will confront those who are representing God or fighting for His plans and purposes. If it comes to visit you, take it as a compliment, because in some way you must be advancing God's kingdom.

His Strategy: Intimidation to Produce Fear

Goliath's main strategy of attack is intimidation. To *intimidate* means "threaten, bully, menace, stand over, terrorize" and "frighten in order to induce and inspire with fear." These definitions capture who Goliath is and what he does. This spirit is just a bully that wants to undermine you and rip away your confidence. As Goliath stood day after day before the Israelite army and declared his challenge to fight, the Bible says:

> *On hearing the Philistine's words, Saul and all the Israelites were dismayed and terrified.... When the Israelites saw the man, they all ran from him in great fear.*
> —1 SAMUEL 17:11, 24

This one giant of a man had disempowered a whole army. Not a single soldier in the Israelite army was courageous enough to stand up and fight against him. You can imagine the atmosphere in the Israelite camp. The whole army was filled with fear and terror, and they felt useless and vulnerable. The key word here is *fear*. The Goliath spirit wants to incite fear into our hearts that will render us insecure and inactive.

His Weapon: Mockery

Goliath was imposing in stature and equipped with impressive armor, but his most powerful weapons were actually the words he spoke. These words were like arrows that had been poisoned with contempt due to his defiant heart. His major weapon of warfare was mockery, and he spoke scornfully and sarcastically to his enemies.

Mockery is characterized by scathing words that bring insult or ridicule. To *mock* means "to scoff, make fun of, put down, and tease." This is exactly what Goliath did to the Israelite army, and this is what the devil will do to you and me.

How many times have I heard the mocking, lying words of the devil resound in my head? They sound something like this: "As if you could do this. As if God would choose you. You're hopeless. If you do this you are certainly going to fail. You're not qualified; there are plenty of other people that can do the job better than you. As if you could have any influence."

These lying words are directed at undermining our identity (who we are) and our purpose (what we can do). The enemy aims to destroy our sense of self. He will do this by making us doubt that we are special and significant. Once these lies infiltrate our heart and our mind they become personal truths that we believe. By far, the top two lies spoken by the devil, which are twisted to become false truths in our lives, are the following:

Lie: "You're no one special." False Truth: "I am nothing."
Lie: "You're no one significant." False Truth: "I have nothing to offer."

I'm sure you are familiar with these lies and the impact they have on your life. These words and the sarcastic tone in which they are uttered are actually the mocking, false accusations of the devil. He verbalizes them boldly or even at times as a whisper, but his aim is always the same. He wants to disempower you by inducing a sense of fear and making you feel useless and worthless, incompetent and ineffective. Ah! How I hate it when even one of these lies pierces my heart.

You have to remember and be alert to the fact that the primary focus and modus operandi of this demonic spirit is to stop you from rising and moving forward. It does not want you to personally grow or for you to advance the kingdom of God. It is hell-bent on keeping you small, insignificant, and stationary.

DAVID: THE HERO

Let's now turn our attention to David, the hero of this story. I love the faith and passion in this young man. He is determined to conquer Goliath because he detests the defying spirit of this giant, and he recognizes that Goliath is not only defying King Saul and the nation of Israel but God himself. David boldly and angrily declares:

> *"Who is this uncircumcised Philistine that he should defy the armies of the living God?"*
>
> —1 SAMUEL 17:26

Circumcision was a procedure that God required of all the Jewish males as a sign and a seal of the covenant God had made with Israel. Circumcision demonstrated Israel's allegiance to God and confirmed that Israel was God's chosen nation.

When David reminded Goliath that he was uncircumcised, he was publicly reminding everyone that Goliath and the rest of the Philistine army were neither special nor significant in the eyes of God. Goliath therefore had no power or authority to contend with the Israelite army, whose soldiers were fighting on the side of the almighty God. David knew this. He had a God-perspective of the situation. Sometimes that's all we need—a shift in perspective to see things from a godly or spiritual viewpoint. That's what David was able to bring to this battle situation, the revelation that one large, skilled, veteran warrior could not possibly win against a smaller, less experienced young man who had the Lord of lords and the King of kings on his side!

David, like Goliath, became consumed with defiance and indignation. His defiance was directed not only at Goliath but at the devil. David became impassioned with a righteous anger, shouting this prophetic declaration of victory:

> David said to the Philistine, *"You come against me with sword and spear and javelin, but I come against you in the name of the LORD Almighty, the God of the armies of Israel, whom you have defied. This day the LORD will hand you over to me, and I'll strike you down and cut off*

your head. Today I will give the carcasses of the Philistine army to the birds of the air and the beasts of the earth, and the whole world will know that there is a God in Israel. All those gathered here will know that it is not by sword or spear that the LORD saves; for the battle is the LORD's, and he will give all of you into our hands.

—1 SAMUEL 17:45–47

David's Strategies and Weapons

If Goliath represents the demonic spirit I saw in my vision, then I must conclude that David represents you and me. It's important then that we understand the strategies and weapons David employed to overcome Goliath so that we can also employ them to overcome this demonic spirit.

Firstly and most importantly, this young man chose to be true to himself. The ruler at the time, King Saul, wanted to dress David in his own royal armor. David tried it on but found he wasn't comfortable in Saul's tunic, coat of armor, helmet, and sword. So David respectfully refused Saul's help. Trained as a shepherd boy, he chose to arm himself with weapons familiar to him: speed, a staff, a sling, and a selection of smooth stones from the stream. It took just one of David's stones, strategically implanted in the middle of Goliath's head, to kill the giant and bring victory to Israel. How important it is to remember that when we fight spiritual battles we must always be true to ourselves. The devil will eat us for breakfast if we are trying to be someone or something we are not.

Secondly, David chose to ignore the derogatory comments and doubting attitudes not only from Goliath but also from those around him. When Eliab, David's eldest brother, realized that his little brother was preparing himself to fight the giant, he cuttingly remarked to David:

Why have you come down here? And with whom did you leave those few sheep in the desert? I know how conceited you are and how wicked your heart is; you came down only to watch the battle.

—1 SAMUEL 17:28

Not only does Eliab belittle David as a mere shepherd boy, he also judges David's motives. David wisely chooses not to allow these comments to intimidate him. He responds directly to Eliab, and then purposefully turns away in order to be out of earshot from hearing any other rude remarks.

Sometimes when we attempt to rise up, it is the people closest to us that are most able to pull us down because they are the ones who best know our weaknesses and insecurities. It is up to us to have strong boundaries and to ignore any negative comments that could squash or dampen our spirits and our efforts. Even King Saul doubted that David could fight Goliath. He said to David:

> *"You are not able to go out against this Philistine and fight him; you are only a boy, and he has been a fighting man from his youth."*
> —1 SAMUEL 17:33

David chose not to be perturbed by his eldest brother or his king. He respected the authority and position of Saul, but this did not stop him from speaking his mind when he did not agree with the king. Many others would have fainted with intimidation. We must maintain respect for authority but not lose ourselves or our voice over what we believe to be true and right.

Thirdly, David gained courage by reflecting upon his previous victories. He had never competed in a battle man to man, but he had often fought against ferocious animals that were attacking his precious sheep. God had previously helped him kill bears and lions, so David could confidently proclaim:

> *"The LORD who delivered me from the paw of the lion and the paw of the bear will deliver me from the hand of this Philistine."*
> —1 SAMUEL 17:37

From a heart filled with faith, David spoke in faith and acted in faith. At the battlefront David declared victory and then took immediate action: he ran toward the giant, took the first shot, and slew him. How quick and how sweet was the victory!

David seized the giant's sword, using it to cut off his head. The entire Philistine army, horrified that their hero was dead, turned and fled. That day, one man's faith brought victory to an entire nation. We may never fully know who and what is on the other side of us pushing through our own personal battles. Our wins will often be a catalyst for other people's victories.

OUR BATTLES

In the midst of our battles we need to allow our spirits to rise and to fight. Most importantly, we need to have the proper perspective: that we have Jesus fighting with us and for us. We are on the winning side because Jesus has already won! When we are opposed by this demonic spirit, it is our responsibility and our right to defy the devil. We need to boldly declare the Word of God and to remind the devil of his place and his future.

The reason the Son of God appeared was to destroy the devil's work.
—1 JOHN 3:8

We know that anyone born of God does not continue to sin; the one who was born of God keeps him safe, and the evil one cannot harm him.
—1 JOHN 5:18

MY STORY

I have encountered this spirit on a number of occasions. It's not something I contend with all the time; rather, it tends to appear when I am birthing something new. Let me give you some examples.

A number of years ago I began teaching a course specifically for women in my church. I was breaking new ground, and the devil didn't like it or like me! One night I found it particularly tough going, as everything technical went wrong. I went to bed that night feeling extremely despondent and discouraged.

I awoke the next morning with a strong personal conviction resounding in my heart: "When I get knocked down, I'll get up again. I don't let anything keep me down." I just kept repeating this declaration over and over to myself until my faith was renewed and I could stand tall again.

In moments like this, I face the devil and say to him with a good dose of defiance, "You might knock me down, but I will get up again! You are not going to keep me down! You are not going to stop me! I will keep going! I will not give up! I will keep moving forward! I will win!"

On another occasion I was feeling really kicked about by the devil, and I asked my husband to pray for me. I wanted him to fight this battle on my behalf. Then, I heard the voice of God clearly saying to me, "Amanda, only you can defeat this spirit!" It took my breath away. But when I reflected on the initial vision and the words God had spoken to me months beforehand, I realized they were along they same lines: "Only the woman herself can push through this spirit."

God, at this time, is calling His daughters to be women who have the same courage and convictions as David. He is challenging us to know our authority and to stand in faith. We must choose today to be women who will accept this call and this challenge. No longer can we allow ourselves to be intimidated and mocked; rather, we must rise and be women who conquer this demonic spirit and defy the devil.

TIME TO REFLECT

- Identify times in your life when you have encountered this demonic spirit. What were the circumstances surrounding this attack? How did this attack make you feel? If you overcame this attack, what did you do?
- What are the lies or words of mockery that this demonic spirit speaks into your life? What truth do you need to stand on in order to counterattack these lies?
- Compare your experiences to the vision that I have described in this chapter and the story of David and Goliath. What are the similarities?
- What qualities did David possess that enabled him to fight Goliath and win?
- Identify what strategies you can put into place now so you will be prepared when you encounter this demonic spirit again in the future.

Chapter Ten

GOD'S RESTRAINTS

I was going to call this chapter "God's Shackles," but I felt a strong rebuke in my spirit and the voice of God saying, "I don't put shackles on." What God impressed upon me in that moment was that shackles indicate bondage, imprisonment, and oppression. He never wants to see His daughters bound up and locked away, unreleased and unfulfilled, so God will never put shackles on us. Only the devil does that.

However, on some occasions in your life you will probably experience what I call "God's Restraints." This is when your loving Father is pulling the reins tight around your life. He is preventing you from moving forward and from fulfilling the vision that is burning deep inside of you. His voice will be saying, "Stop. Not yet!" "Stop. You're not ready!" "Stop. The time is not right!" In this time of *stop*, you will feel the restraining tug of God upon your life.

It's so important that you understand why this happens and how to walk through this time. From my experience, it can be one of the most painful and challenging seasons of life. It often occurs when we are filled with vision and a yearning to launch out and go for it. But in the time of restraint, vision is put on pause. God is saying, "Wait."

THE WAITING TIME AND THE WAITING PLACE

During this waiting time we can experience extreme frustration and even become angry, discouraged, or disappointed with God. It is a place where we may feel hidden and alone. It may also be a time when we deem that neither God nor man notices, promotes, or endorses us. I believe there are a number of reasons why God restrains us and calls us to wait.

Reason 1: Days of Personal Preparation

There is often an extended time period between when a vision is conceived and when the vision is completed. This gap exists because we are often not as big as the vision we carry. To fit and fulfill the dream we have to grow in character, capacity, and capability. It is during this time of growth and preparation that we will often experience the restraining hand of God.

There was a time in my life when I felt hidden and restrained, and God revealed to me a picture that explained the process He was taking me through. He showed me that I was a thoroughbred racing horse being trained to win elite races. I was frustrated because I wanted to be racing. I wanted to be doing what I felt I was called to do. I saw very clearly that I was still frisky, temperamental, and undisciplined. Because of this my trainer was holding me by a harness and taking me through some routine exercises. Immediately this season of my life became clear to me. I still had some rough edges that needed smoothing over before I would be ready to be released to race.

I keep a book of the prophetic words people have spoken into my life, and every now and then I look over them. One day I decided to summarize these prophecies. I discovered a range of interesting words that were all based on a similar theme: *prepared, enlarged, sharpened, trained, tempered, coached, discipled,* and *shaped.* All these words are associated with painful sensations and personal stretching. I have felt that pain and that stretch! I know that for the attainment of the dreams in my life and to fulfill the call for which I am created, I have to go through all the pain and the process of God's preparation. So will you!

Earlier in the book, I shared with you how for a whole year God spoke loudly into my spirit the words *rise up*, and these words were dramatically changed the next year to *grow up*! After a year or two of growing up, I asked God to show me a picture of where He was and what He had been doing in my life. Once again He showed me a vivid image.

I saw God as my coach standing at the top of a tall, steep mountain. I was midway up, climbing toward Him. The going was tough and arduous. I was tired, exhausted, and beyond my physical and emotional limits. God was looking over the mountain toward me and speaking very loud, strong words. He was urging me onward, instilling courage and strength into my being. And He was being far from gentle. God was literally yelling at me these words, "Come on, Amanda. Rise up. You can do it. Come on, keep growing. Come up here!" I knew that He was not going to leave that mountaintop without me. And, yes, I did eventually make it to the summit. Many of you will have experienced similar situations, prophecies, and purposes in God. If we're going to be women whom God can use for His purposes, then we must be ready to be refined, willing to be stretched, and prepared to wait.

Reason 2: Waiting for God-Appointed Times and Purposes

Then the LORD replied: "Write down the revelation and make it plain on tablets so that a herald may run with it. For the revelation awaits an appointed time; it speaks of the end and will not prove false. Though it linger, wait for it; it will certainly come and will not delay."
—HABAKKUK 2:2–3

Everything in God has an appointed purpose and an appointed time. Vision is first revealed at a time chosen by God, and then it is often made to wait. The vision will come to pass at an appointed time in the future, but only God knows this time. It is a time sovereignly chosen by Him when the purpose of the vision will best be fulfilled.

Many years ago I heard a wonderful message by Graham Fletcher, who presently pastors a C3 church in Canada. His message was titled "Hannah Wanted a Baby but God Wanted a Prophet." It was a message describing how God's purposes and Hannah's desire collided and brought forth Samuel. The full story can be read in 1 Samuel 1–3, but here it is in brief.

Hannah was barren. The Bible says that the Lord had closed her womb, thus causing her a great deal of anguish and misery. Apart from dealing with her own personal disappointment and pain, she was constantly provoked and taunted by her husband's other wife, Peninnah. The Bible says it very simply: "Peninnah had children, but Hannah had none" (1 Sam. 1:2). Often when we have an unfulfilled dream, someone very close to us is successful in the area of our greatest desire. This can raise many emotions of insecurity, jealousy, and anger. It is a test to keep us trusting God and believing for the promise He has spoken into our lives.

Hannah was a godly woman, so she took her pain and her plea to God. She was also a wise woman, because she found solace at the temple. It was there that she encountered God's peace and His presence. I love this! Sometimes Christians in this waiting period turn aside from church and from God. But not Hannah. She turned to Him.

> In bitterness of soul Hannah wept much and prayed to the LORD. And she made a vow, saying, "O LORD Almighty, if you will only look upon your servant's misery and remember me, and not forget your servant but give her a son, then I will give him to the LORD for all the days of his life, and no razor will ever be used on his head [a sign of consecration]."
> —1 SAMUEL 1:10–11

I believe this prayer would have brought great delight to the heart of God. He saw and heard all of Hannah's emotion, but it was her faith and devotion that captured His attention. Hannah was willing to hand over the baby, whom she so earnestly longed for, to God and to His purposes. Because of Hannah's vow and sacrifice, God was now able to fulfill His dream and plan: that a priest and prophet would be raised up who would speak to the people of Israel on His behalf.

> I will raise up for myself a faithful priest, who will do according to what is in my heart and mind. I will firmly establish his house, and he will minister before my anointed one always.
> —1 SAMUEL 2:35

How amazing is this story? Hannah wanted a baby. God wanted a prophet. Hannah's womb was closed by God and then opened at the appointed time for His appointed purpose. All the desperation, pain, torment, and grief that Hannah experienced was for a higher cause. She was preparing herself to give birth to Samuel, a prophet who would change the nation of Israel. We do not always know the bigger purpose to the dreams that we carry in our hearts. All we can do is trust God and know that the day will come when the restraints will be eased. Let me reassure you that at the appointed time the "stop" will turn to "go," and the "wait' will be replaced with a resounding "now"!

Reason 3: Learning to Trust God, Our Promise-Maker and Promise-Keeper

The waiting time between when God speaks His promise and when He fulfills them in our life is the time we learn to trust the power and integrity of God's character and His Word. We have to discover that God is not only our Promise-Maker but also our Promise-Keeper. Here are some scriptures that I've personally found helpful in the midst of waiting for the promises of God to be fulfilled in my own life.

God is not a man, that he should lie, nor a son of man, that he should change his mind. Does he speak and then not act? Does he promise and not fulfill?

—NUMBERS 23:19

You have kept your promise to your servant David my father; with your mouth you have promised and with your hand you have fulfilled it—as it is today.

—1 KINGS 8:24

The LORD Almighty has sworn, "Surely, as I have planned, so it will be, and as I have purposed, so it will stand."

—ISAIAH 14:24

As the rain and the snow come down from heaven, and do not return to it without watering the earth and making it bud and flourish, so that it yields seed for the sower and bread for the eater, so is my word that goes out from my mouth: It will not return to me empty, but will accomplish what I desire and achieve the purpose for which I sent it.

—ISAIAH 55:10–11

But as surely as God is faithful, our message to you is not "Yes" and "No." For the Son of God, Jesus Christ, who was preached among you by me and Silas and Timothy, was not "Yes" and "No," but in him it has always been "Yes." For no matter how many promises God has made, they are "Yes" in Christ. And so through him the "Amen" is spoken by us to the glory of God.

—2 Corinthians 1:18–20

These scriptures assure me of a number of things:

- The words God has spoken into my life are actually promises.
- If God makes me a promise, He will also make sure it is fulfilled.
- God speaks promises with His mouth, but it is His hands that will fulfill them.
- What God promises is always valid because He does not lie or change His mind.
- Nothing can change God's promises, plans, and purposes.
- God watches over His promises to ensure they are accomplished.
- What God says He will do, He will do.
- Every promise God has spoken is "yes" and "amen;" therefore, they will all happen. They will come to completion.

This waiting period is not only a time when our emotions can be challenged but also our very faith and trust in God. Abraham, our father in the faith, had to wait a long, long, long time until the word spoken to him was fulfilled. God promised Abraham that from his body a whole nation would be born. When this promise was spoken, Abraham did not even have one child with his wife Sarah, and it remained this way for another twenty-five long years. So what did Abraham do? He chose to believe! He focused his thoughts and his faith on images that reminded him of his future descendants. At night Abraham stared at the stars, and by day he studied the grains of the sand. In his heart, he held on to the promise!

The apostle Paul was able to make these statements about Abraham's faith:

By faith Abraham . . . was enabled to become a father because he considered him faithful who had made the promise.

—Hebrews 11:11

He did not waver through unbelief regarding the promise of God, but was strengthened in his faith and gave glory to God, being fully persuaded that God had power to do what he had promised.

—ROMANS 4:20–21

Like Abraham, we can also be assured that God is both faithful and powerful to fulfill the things He has promised us. In the midst of waiting and restraint, we must choose to trust the one who is both our Promise-Maker and our Promise-Keeper.

Reason 4: The Dream Must Die

I believe the final reason God restrains us and makes us wait is that sometimes the vision we carry can become more important to us than our relationship with God. Our focus and our heart can become shifted away from Him and onto our own desires and vision. We must understand that God is a jealous God; He requires that He is number one in our hearts. If something steals our affection, then it has become our Lord and even our idol. This can happen with a relationship, the pursuit of an ambition, a material possession, or even an unfulfilled dream. When this occurs in our life, God commonly asks us to die to our self and to our dreams. We need to respond by repenting and making a decision to never allow the dream to distract our hearts and steal our affections from Jesus, our first love.

The dying process is a painful one. There have been a number of times when God has called me to die to myself and die to my dreams. On one occasion I literally buried my dreams. I wrote them down on a piece of paper, dug a hole in the ground, covered them in soil, and spoke aloud to them this single word: *die.* Other times, in my heart and imagination, I have stabbed my dreams with a big sword or pinned them and myself to the cross. Dying is a time when we consecrate our lives afresh to God and we seek to find a place of contentment and joy, even when our dreams and call are not being realized. In this season of waiting, unfruitfulness, and death, take heart from these words of the prophet Habakkuk:

Though the fig tree does not bud and there are no grapes on the vines, though the olive crop fails and the fields produce no food, though there are no sheep in the pen and no cattle in the stalls, yet I will rejoice in the LORD, I will be joyful in God my Savior.

—HABAKKUK 3:17–18

THE WAITING TIME IN DAVID'S LIFE

You have probably guessed by now that I love David; he is one of my most favorite people in the Bible. I love his heart, his calling, his strengths, his weaknesses, his passion for worship, his psalms, his zeal for the temple, and his devotion to God. During one period of my life I reread his story in the light of gaining revelation about what David did during the waiting time of his life, the time when God was preparing him to be king of Israel. Let me share with you what I discovered.

David was only fifteen years old when Samuel came to visit his home and his father, Jesse. The prophet had been given instructions by God to anoint one of Jesse's sons as the nation's future king. Jesse had eight sons, and one by one the sons lined up in front of Samuel to see if they would be the son chosen to be the next king of Israel. One by one Samuel said, "No, not this one." After doing this seven times Samuel was rather perplexed, because he knew that God had sent him to this family but as yet he had not found the next heir to the throne. David was absent from the house because Jesse had not considered his youngest son a suitable candidate. As a shepherd boy, David was still out in the paddocks tending his flock of sheep. When Samuel was informed of this, he said, "Send for him; we will not sit down until he arrives" (1 Sam. 16:11).

It was out there in the paddocks that David had caught God's attention. God had noticed that David was a responsible young man who lovingly cared for the needs of his sheep. God could foresee David would be a man who would faithfully guide and govern the people of Israel. It was out there in the paddocks that God saw David courageously fight the lions and bears that would attack and kill his sheep. God could see that David, in the future, would be a mighty warrior who would fight Goliath and kill many enemies of Israel. It was out there in the paddocks that David captured God's heart by praying and lifting his voice in worship. This caused God to say that yes, here was a man whom He would anoint to be king, through whose descendants would come His Son, Jesus, the Savior of the world.

David was eventually brought before Samuel, and the Lord said, "Rise and anoint him; he is the one" (1 Sam. 16:12). At this point in time God chose and anointed David to be the next king of Israel. However, it was another fifteen long years before David was anointed by man to this same position. In 2 Samuel 5:3–4 we read, "When all the elders of Israel had come to King David at Hebron, the king made a compact with them at Hebron before the Lord, and they anointed David king over Israel. David was thirty years old when he became king, and he reigned forty years."

I have discovered there is often a big gap or a long period of time between when God appoints and anoints you to a position and when man appoints and anoints you to this same position. This is the way God works. He calls us first, and then He makes us. After we have been made, others recognize the gifting and call on our life, and then they commission us to fulfill that call.

So what did David do in the fifteen years when he carried this dream and this call? I am sure there were times when he doubted God and himself. I am sure there would have been occasions when he felt alone and hidden. He would have gone through every emotion imaginable, especially as he was chosen to serve Saul, the mad king he was going to replace. There were even two instances when he could have killed Saul to give himself a quick route to the throne. But David refused! He chose to wait and trust God. Surely David understood that he was in days of preparation when his character and faith were being strengthened and his leadership skills sharpened.

Shortly after David was anointed by Samuel, he moved on from shepherding sheep and began to lead people. He banded together a few disgruntled men. "All those who were in distress or in debt or discontented gathered around him, and he became their leader. About four hundred men were with him" (1 Sam. 22:2). Only one chapter later we see that David's party was growing in number and might. By then he had six hundred men (1 Sam. 23:13). The Bible enlightens us to David's increasing influence: "David grew stronger and stronger, while the house of Saul grew weaker and weaker" (2 Sam. 3:1). On another occasion the Scriptures state, "He became more and more powerful, because the Lord God Almighty was with him" (2 Sam. 5:10).

During those fifteen years David led his men in battles against the enemies of Israel and he displayed wisdom, courage, and strength. He had a reputation for "slaying tens of thousands." In 1 Chronicles 12:23–37 there is a list of all the men who came from different areas of the nation to join forces with David. The total was a staggering 340,822 men. No longer was David gathering the down-and-outs, but rather brave and mighty men who were fiercely loyal to him. One of his chief warriors made this declaration, which reflected the spirit of all the men:

> *"We are yours, O David! We are with you, O son of Jesse! Success, success to you, and success to those who help you."*
> —1 CHRONICLES 12:18

Why were David's men so loyal? I believe it is because David sowed loyalty. He was fiercely faithful and dedicated to King Saul. He respected Saul's position and the fact that God had placed and anointed him as king. Saul was insecure, possessed by an evil spirit, sought advice from a witch, and tried to kill David on a number of occasions; however, David continued to serve, honor, and esteem him.

The Bible says, "In everything he did he had great success, because the LORD was with him" (1 Sam. 18:14). Not only was the Lord with David, but more importantly David was with the Lord. We see in the psalms how David's heart was inclined to prayer and worship. When in battle and faced with life and death decisions, David would always stop and seek the Lord for strength, guidance, and wisdom. We also read that when David was in the pit of despair he would pour out his heart to God. During these times of trouble David discovered that God was his refuge, his fortress, and his helper. He knew without a doubt that the source of his success was his relationship with God.

Let me summarize what happened in David's life during the fifteen years he had to prepare and wait to be crowned the king of Israel:

- David's revelation of God was enlarged;
- his faith was strengthened;
- David's character was tested and refined;
- his leadership capabilities and capacity were broadened;

- David learned to trust and revere God no matter what the circumstance;
- he rose as a mighty warrior; and
- David gained the honor and esteem of the nation of Israel.

I want to finish this chapter with an exhortation from King David. These are insightful words about what to do in the days of preparation and the times of waiting.

Trust in the LORD and do good; dwell in the land and enjoy safe pasture. Delight yourself in the LORD and he will give you the desires of your heart. Commit your way to the LORD; trust in him and he will do this: He will make your righteousness shine like the dawn, the justice of your cause like the noonday sun. Be still before the LORD and wait patiently for him;

—PSALM 37:3–7

- Identify if there have been any times in your life when you have felt the restraining pull of God. Why do you think He was restraining you?
- Identify dreams you have had that have taken time to be fulfilled. Why do you think there was a gap between when you conceived the dream and when you completed the dream?
- Have you ever had to die to yourself or to your dream? Why, and what process did you go through when you did this?
- After reading about David and how he walked through the waiting time in his life, what did you learn and how can you apply this to your own life?

liberating truth

Chapter Eleven

TRUTH REVEALED

Ignorance and deception have kept women imprisoned and unreleased for centuries. In many churches and communities naivety and confusion reign over such questions as:

- Are men and women equal?
- Are men superior to women?
- Do women have to submit to all men or just to their husbands?
- Is submission a subservient role?
- Are women able to prophesy, teach, and preach?
- Can women lead churches or be an apostle?

It is vital that both men and women clearly understand what the Bible says about the value, status, and roles of women. It is important that we take the time to discover this truth and be challenged about our own beliefs and attitudes. I am utterly convinced that the devil has allowed Scripture to be misinterpreted and misunderstood. This incorrect teaching has undermined women by demeaning who they are and what they can do. It is not until biblical truth is fully revealed, understood, and applied that women will be empowered to rise and fulfill their call and their potential.

The aim of this chapter is to address these questions and reveal truth. We will do this by taking a walk through the Bible. I want to say up front but unapologetically that this chapter is more what I would call a teaching chapter. If you have just snuggled into bed and are a bit sleepy, I would probably recommend you come back to this chapter at a later time. But make sure you do come back. The truth will not only enlighten you, it might just surprise you!

CREATION: GOD'S ORIGINAL INTENT

So God created man in his own image, in the image of God he created him; male and female he created them. God blessed them and said to them, "Be fruitful and increase in number; fill the earth and subdue it. Rule over the fish of the sea and the birds of the air and over every living creature that moves on the ground."

—GENESIS 1:27–28

Both men and women were created in the image of God and both were given authority to rule and be fruitful. They were created male and female: alike but different, individuals but interdependent. Adam was created first by God, and I find it amazing that although he walked with the Lord in the Garden of Eden, the Bible says he was alone. This man was actually incomplete without a woman. So God fashioned a woman out of the rib of the man to be his beautiful companion, partner, and helper in life. She not only reflected the image of God but also the image of the man. I love these quotations from a number of different Bible commentaries highlighting the relationship between man and woman, including their equality of value and worth.

God could have formed the woman out of the dust of the earth, as he had formed the man; but had he done so, she must have appeared in his eyes as a distinct being, to whom he had no natural relation. But as God formed her out of a part of the man himself, he saw she was of the same nature, the same identical flesh and blood, and of the same constitution in all respects, and consequently having equal powers, faculties, and rights. This at once ensured his affection, and excited his esteem.

—ADAM CLARKE COMMENTARY[1]

That the woman was made of a rib out of the side of Adam; not made out of his head to rule over him, nor out of his feet to be trampled upon by him, but out of his side to be equal with him, under his arm to be protected, and near his heart to be beloved.

—MATTHEW HENRY COMMENTARY[2]

The Authority Question

One of the more controversial and misunderstood topics in the church today regards authority, and in particular the issues of headship and submission. Women nowadays who live in cultures with prevailing feminist views either disregard the fundamental command to submit to their husbands or live perplexed about how they successfully apply this instruction to their own lives and marriages.

I believe the roles of headship and submission in the marriage union were instituted by God during Creation. I want to reiterate here that God created men and women equal. However, in marriage the position and roles of the man and the woman are different. Let's have a look at these insightful words from Dwight Pratt:

> *She is man's complement, essential to the perfection of his being. Without her he is not man in the generic fullness of that term. Priority of creation may indicate headship, but not, as theologians have so uniformly affirmed, superiority. Dependence indicates difference of function, not inferiority. Human values are estimated in terms of the mental and spiritual. Man and woman are endowed for equality, and are mutually interdependent.*[3]

Pratt states it beautifully: men and women are mutually interdependent; that is, they need each other. He highlights the fact that God created them with equal ability, capacity, and standing. Neither gender, he claims, is superior or inferior to the other. Pratt also notes that the position of headship was bestowed upon the man by God.

Let me point out here that headship between a man and a woman only applies in the context of marriage. In the church and in society, the issues of headship and submission are not based on gender but rather on the positions people hold. Let me explain this further. Here on Earth, there are three institutions that God has established, and they have their own unique authority structure. They are:

1. the society in which we live
2. the church

3. the marriage relationship and the family

In each of these three structures, certain people are appointed to be the head and to lead, and others are required to submit and to follow. In society men and women are deemed by God to be equally significant and gifted and should be allowed to have equal opportunities, rights, and privileges. Power and the responsibility to rule are given to those who have been elected or appointed to positions of authority. This includes governmental leaders, our bosses, our teachers, and organizations that administer the rules and regulations of the land. The Bible says that everyone must submit to, respect, and obey those who govern and lead them. In society, both men and women are capable to lead or are called to submit. Position is not dependent on gender but rather on ability and appointed authority.

Everyone must submit himself to the governing authorities, for there is no authority except that which God has established. The authorities that exist have been established by God. Consequently, he who rebels against the authority is rebelling against what God has instituted, and those who do so will bring judgment on themselves.

—ROMANS 13:1–2

Slaves, submit yourselves to your masters with all respect, not only to those who are good and considerate, but also to those who are harsh.

—1 PETER 2:18

Let's take a look now at a passage of scripture that outlines the issues of headship and submission in the context of church and marriage.

Submit to one another out of reverence for Christ. Wives, submit to your husbands as to the Lord. For the husband is the head of the wife as Christ is the head of the church, his body, of which he is the Savior. Now as the church submits to Christ, so also wives should submit to their husbands in everything. Husbands, love your wives, just as Christ loved the church and gave himself up for her to make her holy, cleansing her by the washing with water through the word, and to present her to himself as a radiant church, without stain or wrinkle or any other blemish, but holy and blameless. In this same way, husbands ought to love their wives

176

as their own bodies. He who loves his wife loves himself.... However, each one of you also must love his wife as he loves himself, and the wife must respect her husband.

—Ephesians 5:21–28, 33

This scripture states that Jesus is the Head of the church. The church includes every believer, whether they are male or female, young or old. In the church the two genders are of equal standing. All men and all women are to submit to Christ, who is the Head of the church. We are also required to submit to one another as brothers and sisters in the Lord. Furthermore, both men and women are expected by God to submit to the leaders in their own churches. Authority within the church is based on calling and whom God anoints and appoints to governmental positions. God will place men or women into these leadership positions, and whoever is under the authority of these leaders must submit to them no matter what their gender.

Remember your leaders, who spoke the word of God to you. Consider the outcome of their way of life and imitate their faith.... Obey your leaders and submit to their authority. They keep watch over you as men who must give an account. Obey them so that their work will be a joy, not a burden, for that would be of no advantage to you.

—Hebrews 13:7, 17

Let's look now at how the principles of headship and submission work in domestic relationships. In the marriage union women are required to submit to the headship of a man, and this man is her husband. I have found this is where the confusion abounds! Many people have not understood that the institution of marriage is a distinct entity with its own unique authority structure. Consequently, God's instructions regarding the marriage relationship have been wrongly applied to the church and to society. For example, many have falsely argued that men are the head over all women; therefore, all women are obligated to submit to all men. A further fallacy that pervades many cultures is the notion that because man is the head, then he is superior to the woman. I want to emphatically declare that neither of these assertions is the case. Just because God has ordained the position and roles in marriage to be different does not mean that women are inferior or have any less value or worth than men.

Let me give you an example of how the authority question is answered in my own life. As a woman I submit to the authorities who govern me in my community and nation where I live. In my church I submit to the authority of my pastors. As a wife, I submit to my husband. Here is another example. In our movement of churches, we have some women who have been appointed by God to be the senior pastor of a church. In this situation the husbands are not employed by the church because they are gifted by God to work in other fields. This means that the woman is the one who has the responsibility of governing the church. In a situation like this, the woman submits to her husband within her marriage. However, in the context of church, the husband and the other men and women in the congregation are required to submit to her leadership.

Understanding Headship and Submission

Another area of difficulty lies in understanding what it means to be the head and to submit. Headship is a position instituted by God; it determines who will lead and hold ultimate authority and responsibility. Christ is the Head or the Leader of the church, just as in the marriage relationship the husband is the head and the leader. In this role the husband must make wise decisions, give direction, and provide protection for his marriage and his family.

We can note from the passage we read earlier in Ephesians 5 that Christ leads the church with love. Jesus actually demonstrated true headship and leadership by becoming a servant. His love toward the church was always kind and self-sacrificing. The scripture says that Jesus "gave himself up for her" and He "feeds and cares" for the church (v. 25, 29). This is the way God shows husbands how to be the head and to lead their wives. Following Jesus' example, Christian men need to value, nurture, empower, and "love their wives as their own bodies" (v. 28). This must be the foundation and the motivation from which husbands lead in their marriages.

Too many people for too long have regarded headship as a master-and-servant relationship, more like a dictatorship, where to lead means to rule and obedience is a requirement. But the Bible doesn't tell wives to obey their husbands; they are told to submit. Children are required to obey their parents, servants are commanded to obey their masters, believers are directed to obey their leaders, but wives are called to submit to their husbands. Submission is different from obedience.

> *Wives, submit to your husbands, as is fitting in the Lord. Husbands, love your wives and do not be harsh with them. Children, obey your parents in everything, for this pleases the Lord. Fathers, do not embitter your children, or they will become discouraged. Slaves, obey your earthly masters in everything.*
>
> —COLOSSIANS 3:18–22

Obedience is mandatory and a matter of duty. It requires conformity and compliance to laws, instructions, or orders. There is no indication from Scripture that the husband, as the head, has a right to give commands or orders or to demand obedience from his wife. The role of the husband, therefore, is different from the position of a parent, master, or boss. The foundation from which a husband leads must always be kindness and servanthood. The ultimate marriage union is one in which the husband chooses to lovingly lead and the wife chooses to respectfully submit.

Unlike *obedience*, the word *submission* implies that the wife actually has a free will or a choice. A wife who submits has recognized and accepted that her husband has been appointed by God to be her head. She responds to her husband, then, from this position of revelation and decision. *Submission* literally means "to yield." In my words, it is about flowing and following! Submission recognizes that under one roof you cannot have two leaders. It's about having an approach of cooperation rather than contention and having a heart that desires unity rather than division. In Bible times the word *submit* applied to "a voluntary attitude of giving in, cooperating, assuming responsibility, and carrying a burden."

Interestingly, God requires women to submit to their husbands whether they are believers or nonbelievers. This highlights the fact that as wives we are called to esteem the God-ordained position of "head." I believe that to submit to our husbands is actually an act of obedience to the Lord. This scripture also clearly states that wives who choose to submit will actually win their unsaved husbands to the Lord. Now, that is powerful!

Wives, in the same way be submissive to your husbands so that, if any of them do not believe the word, they may be won over without words by the behavior of their wives, when they see the purity and reverence of your lives.

—1 PETER 3:1–2

Many wives become perplexed about what it means for their husband to be their head and how they should submit. I have heard these questions asked by many women:

- Does this mean I have to be quiet, meek, and mild?
- Do I lose control of my life?
- Am I allowed to have an opinion?
- Can I voice my wishes and argue my case?
- Why should I respect him when he makes unwise decisions and behaves poorly?

Let me share with you how submission works in my marriage. Pat and I consider that we are partners living and working together as a team; therefore, we discuss every aspect of our life. My husband loves and respects me, so he wants to know my needs and hear my thoughts, opinions, and ideas. We make all our decisions together. In twenty years of marriage I can only remember a few times when we have disagreed with each other. On these rare occasions I have chosen to voluntarily submit and allow my husband to make the final call.

Have I found this easy? Mostly not, because I have a healthy ego! However, many years ago I made a decision that I would be a wife who respects the position of "head" that has been given to my husband by God and that I would submit to his leadership. The power of a predetermined decision is amazing; you can decide now how you will respond to something you will face in the future. I have found that in those occasions when I disagreed with my husband but chose to submit to his decision, remarkably things have always turned out for the best—both for me and for our marriage. I know that God honors a woman who submits to her husband.

The Bible encourages us to be submissive like Sarah, the wife of Abraham. It's interesting to read the Book of Genesis and to see how Sarah behaved with her husband. The first thing that strikes me when I look at their marriage relationship is that Abraham treated his wife with respect. They were partners in life. Together they obeyed God and moved their family to the land God had promised Abraham, and together they walked the journey of waiting twenty-five years to conceive Isaac, their first child and the seed of the Israelite nation.

On one occasion while they were traveling, Abraham asked his wife to pretend that she was his sister. He feared that the foreigners would steal her away because she was so beautiful. Interestingly, Sarah complied with this request, even though it could have put her life in even more danger. In another incident, Sarah was in conflict over Abraham's concubine and son. Sarah openly discussed her concerns with Abraham, and she actually did this in a very feisty manner. Abraham heard her complaint and then made decisions according to her wishes. (See Genesis 16.) If Sarah is our example to follow of being a submissive wife, I don't think we have to fear!

The Greek word for "submit" is *hupotasso*. It's a military term meaning "to place in right order." It actually indicates the correct arrangement of troops under the command of a leader when they move into battle. I believe any marriage is open to greater spiritual attack when the wife fails to submit. On the other hand, when a wife has chosen submission as a foundational value and behavior in her marriage, she places her marriage relationship in good stead against any attack of the enemy. Headship and submission is not only the right order but the right strategy for keeping your marriage safe and strong.

> *The headship of the husband is paired with the submission of the wife. The interaction of these two creates a relational climate in which a Christian marriage flourishes.*

> —SUE AND LARRY RICHARDS[4]

What Does It Mean to Be My Husband's Helper?

In the beginning, God created man and woman to be companions and partners in life. The woman was also fashioned to be the man's helper. It has been believed and argued by many that the position of helper is an inferior role. This term *helper*, as used in the Scriptures, is actually a term of strength. The Bible says that God is our Helper. It would be foolish for us to think that when God helps us He has become lower or weaker than us. God helps you and me by coming alongside us with His enabling power and grace. That is what a husband and wife team can do for each other.

During the time I was engaged to Pat, I read many books on the topic of marriage. My desire was to gain knowledge, wisdom, and revelation about how to have a great marriage and be an amazing wife. I still vividly remember the day when I first encountered the truth that, as a wife, I was created to be my husband's helper. I actually felt an overwhelming sense of privilege and purpose that I was designed by God to be Pat's helper. In that moment of revelation, I made a commitment before God that I would be the best helper to my one and only husband-to-be, Patrick Antcliff.

You may be wondering how this decision works in my life on an emotional and practical level. I know that I both complement and supplement Pat. I help him to achieve his dreams and his call by praying for him and releasing him. I appreciate who he is and what he does. When he is down, I encourage him. When he has won, we celebrate. I have packed my bags to live overseas to follow the dream in his heart. I have stepped out in faith when he has felt led by God to start businesses. I do the little things that make life more pleasant and easier for him. I do them all because I love him, and I am fulfilling a part of my purpose in life—to be his helper!

I have always appreciated and tried to live by a definition of *submission* that I heard many years ago when I was a new wife: "Submission is submitting to the mission of your husband." I love this! As a wife I have always made a conscious choice to know, support, and release my husband in his mission. I find it a sad phenomenon that many wives do not know what is in the heart of their husbands. It's so important that we identify and support the dreams, the call, and the work of our husbands. I have found this to be my role but also my joy, my privilege, and my freedom.

I deliberately choose the word *freedom* because I am sensing that some of you are still thinking to yourselves, "Yuck. It sounds like a second-class role." Let me just say that in God this principle applies: when you serve others, you will not only be blessed but also honored and promoted by God.

I have found two things to be true: First, because I help my husband, he helps me. Everything I have mentioned that I do for Pat, he also does for me. We are a team. We are partners. We help each other, and that makes our marriage strong and unified. Second, I have found that because I have chosen to be my husband's helper, God chooses to help me. I have seen time and time again, both in my own life and in the lives of other women, that if we put our husband's dreams and desires first, then God will see that ours will also be fulfilled. When we release our husbands to rise, then we too will be released to rise.

THE FALL

The Fall did immense harm to the original intention of God for men and women to be equal partners in ruling the earth. The unity and partnership of Eden gave way to division and domination.

—JOHN FINKELDE[5]

I am hoping that by now you have a clear understanding of God's original intent when He created man and woman and the marriage union. Sadly, when the Fall occurred in Genesis 3, the original order of creation was radically changed. Adam failed to effectively lead and communicate God's instructions to his wife. Eve, on the other hand, used her influence to lead Adam astray and into disobedience. The consequences of the Fall, which Adam and all mankind would now endure, were death, decay, and degradation, both of their physical bodies and of the ground from which they were created. The consequence for Eve and all womankind was an unhealthy need to find a sense of self in men rather than in God.

To the woman he said… "Your desire will be for your husband, and he will rule over you."

—GENESIS 3:16

As we can see, the gender roles for both men and women became horribly broken and distorted in the Fall. A significant consequence was that husbands would now rule over their wives and that women would become subservient and subordinate to the men they had married. The husband, rather than leading his partner with love, would now have dominion or power over her. The wife, on the other hand, lost her power to voluntarily submit to her husband because she was now obliged to obey. Interestingly, her affections and desires also shifted from God on to men. Since the Fall, women have sought to find their sense of value and identity through gaining the approval and favor of men rather than from their Maker. These consequences are far-reaching; however, they do not have to apply to all people and for all time.

The fragmentation of the gender roles that occurred during the Fall has had a dire impact on many cultures and communities throughout the world. When wives and women are ruled over by their husbands or men, they are often subjected to oppressive, abusive, and autocratic authority. The pervasive belief in these societies, institutions, and families is that women are not of equal significance or standing. Therefore, their position and status is one of inferiority and servitude. This is reflected in western cultures by the alarmingly high rates of domestic violence and sexual abuse. In the book *Every Woman in the Bible,* there are some insightful comments about the consequences of the Fall and the impact it has had on the status of women and relationships.

The new state of male domination is regarded as a deterioration of the human condition that resulted from defiance of the divine will…The critical question is, does "He shall rule over you" express God's will for male-female relationships, or does it simply describe the distortion of God's will which sin introduced into our human race? If the latter, the many expressions of male domination in our own and other societies are clearly wrongs perpetrated against women by men.[6]

The Fall twisted Adam and Eve's very nature out of the shape that God had created, warping every dimension of the human personality. For Eve this meant that she and her daughters would find themselves wanting and needing male approval. In this vulnerable state she would be ruled by her husband, not because she was inferior, but because sin had corrupted the relationship between men and women as it had all things. The relationship of complete equality that Adam and Eve had known was altered and since the Fall human societies have reflected the dominant and all too often oppressive rule of men over women.[7]

There is an important distinction to be made in relation to the Fall, and that is the difference between a curse and a consequence. When we look carefully at the verdicts spoken by God, the term *curse* is used only twice, in connection to the serpent and to the earth. In Bible language a curse signifies both a punishment and a binding act. This means that we won't be seeing either the snake grow legs or an easing of the hard work required to farm food from the earth.

On the other hand, the pronouncements that God made to the woman signify consequences. A consequence indicates cause and effect, or the implications of something. It is not a curse. Therefore these verdicts are neither a penalty or a punishment or something which must remain true and firm forever. There can be a return to God's original intent. One of the magnificent truths of the gospel is that Jesus died to restore and redeem not only our connection to the Father but also the relationships between men and women.

WOMEN IN BIBLE TIMES

The life of women in Bible times was very different from the life of women today, especially in the western world. Let me give you a snapshot of what it was like for women back in the days when Jesus walked the Earth.

Women spent most of their time in the seclusion of their homes; they normally did not appear in public settings unless accompanied by an older, trusted male. The head male of the household was legally and economically responsible for the women in his family. A young woman "belonged" to her father, and she was under his authority. He was to provide protection and direction for his daughter. When she married, this young woman then "belonged" to her husband. She was required to obey her husband as she would a master. Whether she was a daughter or a wife, the woman's situation could only be described as restricted and dependant.

Mothers trained their daughters in skills such as spinning, weaving, sewing, cooking, and managing the home. Some girls were also taught basic reading and writing. The usual age for a girl's betrothal was around twelve, and she commonly married a relative. The focus of the wife's duties was her family and the home. Her chief function was to bear children, especially boys; daughters were deemed considerably less valuable than sons.

Society was organized along patriarchal lines. The laws and customs favored men. Aristotle, a preeminent Greek philosopher of that time, believed "the male is by nature superior and the female inferior, the male ruler and the female subject."[8] It was generally regarded that women were weak-minded and fragile. They were commonly treated as objects that men experienced rather than as people in their own right. A man could make demands upon a woman, but a woman could not make demands on a man.

The rights and privileges of women during Bible times were also limited. For example, in a court of law a woman's testimony was deemed invalid unless it was verified by a man, and only a husband had the power to initiate divorce. Jewish women were not required to go to services at the temple. If they did attend, the women had to sit separately from the men, and they were banned from participating in worship. Eliezer, a first-century rabbi, revealed the Jewish attitude toward women learning and being taught the Scriptures: "Rather should the words of the Torah [Jewish scripture] be burned than entrusted to a woman."[9]

Despite these cultural beliefs and traditions, bonds of affection and respect did exist between some husbands and their wives, and between fathers and daughters. Even in these male-dominated and patriarchal cultures it was still possible for women to experience some personal freedom and to rise to prominence. Throughout the Old and New Testaments, we see the following women who were noteworthy for their character, gifts, and faith or for the influential position they held in the church or society.

- Deborah was an influential political leader (Judges 4–5).
- Miriam, Huldah, Anna, and the four daughters of Philip were prophetesses (Exod.15:20; 2 Chron. 34:22–28; Luke 2:36–38; Acts 21:8–9).
- Jael (Judges 4–5) and Esther (Esther 1–5) were nation-deliverers.
- Ruth was a woman of integrity and a faithful and devoted daughter-in-law.

- Hannah was a woman of prayer and devotion to God (1 Sam. 1–2).
- Abigail was noted as a woman of beauty and wisdom (1 Sam. 25).
- Rahab (Josh. 2) and the Shunammite women (2 Kings 4) are remembered for their faith.
- The Proverbs 31 woman was renowned for her prudence, strength, and virtue.
- A group of women financially supported Jesus (Luke 8:3).
- Tabitha (also known as Dorcas) was known for her charitable deeds (Acts 9:36).
- Lydia is a wonderful example of a wealthy businesswoman and a worshiper of God (Acts 16:14–15).
- There were prominent, wealthy, and influential women in the Greek cities of Thessalonica and Berea (Acts 17:4, 12).
- Priscilla was a church leader and teacher of the Word (Acts 18:24–26; Rom. 16:3).
- Phoebe was a servant and deaconess in the church (Rom. 16:1).
- Junia was an apostle and church leader (Rom. 16:7).
- Mary, Tryphena, Tryphosa, and Persis were honored by Paul as hard workers in the church (Rom. 16:6, 12).
- Lois and Eunice were praised for their mentoring role in Timothy's life (2 Tim. 1:5).

JESUS AND WOMEN

During His time on Earth, Jesus acted in ways contrary to popular religious and cultural thinking by compassionately, respectfully, and favorably interacting with women. His actions were revolutionary. He was able to remove some of the rigid structure and restrictions without radically changing the traditional female and male roles. Jesus not only esteemed women but also enlarged their possibilities for a richer life.

What did Jesus do that was radical? He spoke to women in public places. He treated women with value, respect, and grace. He showed genuine concern for the needs of women. He allowed women to touch Him. He fought for the life of an adulterous woman. He welcomed Mary to sit at his feet and be taught the Word of God. He received financial support from women. He allowed women to anoint Him with oil and perfume. He welcomed women to be coworkers in His ministry.

Throughout the Gospels, Jesus purposefully related to women in a manner contrary to what was culturally acceptable. For example, women were the ones who first visited the tomb and witnessed the resurrected Jesus. They were also the first to announce that Jesus had risen and was alive. This was ironic in a nation where the word of a woman was often disregarded and disrespected. Jesus even rebuked the male disciples who failed to believe the women's testimony (Mark 16:9–14).

I would argue that one of the reasons why Jesus came to planet Earth was to restore the status of women and the relationship between the sexes that had been damaged in the Fall and that pervaded Hebrew culture. Jesus' life, death, and resurrection enabled the redemption of both men and women to God's original intent.

I love these insightful thoughts by John Finkelde regarding Jesus' stance on the male chauvinistic culture of Bible times and the secular feminist culture prevalent in many western societies.

> *Christ came to establish Kingdom culture which is the radical middle between these extremes. Kingdom culture neither suppresses nor dominates, rather it celebrates male and female partnership. A partnership of mutual love, mutual equality and mutual service.*[10]

THE SIGNIFICANCE OF PENTECOST

In the last days, God says, I will pour out my Spirit on all people. Your sons and daughters will prophesy, your young men will see visions, your old men will dream dreams. Even on my servants, both men and women, I will pour out my Spirit in those days, and they will prophesy.
—ACTS 2:17–18

On the day of Pentecost, which we read about in Acts 2, the Holy Spirit was poured out on the men and women who were present in the upper room, and supernatural gifts were sovereignly distributed to all without preference to gender. This was a wonderful day of liberation for mankind and woman-kind. With the coming of the Holy Spirit and the birthing of the church, no longer was calling and ministry confined to just one nation (Israel), one tribe (Levites), one gender (male), one man (the high priest), and one day (the Sabbath day). Now "all men and all women, of all tribes and tongues, on all days of the year, can enter the presence of the Lord. They can receive His Spirit and minister prophetically in His name and this power."[11]

On this significant day, equality returned. Now men and women of any age, race, or social status were equally called, equipped, anointed, and gifted to minister in the body of Christ.

> *There is neither Jew nor Greek, slave nor free, male nor female, for you are all one in Christ Jesus.*
>
> —GALATIANS 3:28

PAUL AND HIS VIEW OF WOMEN

Contrary to the opinion of some, the apostle Paul highly esteems women in society, in marriage, and in ministry. His views are far from conventional or conservative. In fact, some of them were radical and in opposition with the thinking of the day. Let's have a look at a number of Paul's beliefs and teachings on each of these subjects.

Women in Society

Paul challenged the Jewish and pagan thinking on patriarchy, the social system where men are dominant and are regarded as the authority within the family and society. At that time, it was commonly believed that the husband, father, or master was above or superior to the rest of society. Women, children, and slaves were not highly valued and were deemed to exist only to serve the man's desires and provide for his needs; they owed a duty of obedience to the male, but he owed no duty to them.

Paul expounded a viewpoint that contrasted with the traditional attitudes in those patriarchal societies. He challenged the men that they, too, had certain responsibilities that they must perform. Paul said that the husband, father, or master is the head of the house; however, he is as responsible to serve the members of his household as they are to serve him. He emphasized that the other members of the household were important and valuable, and therefore needed to be treated with respect and kindness. Paul challenged the men that as a husband, father, or master they had duties toward their wife, children, or slaves, just as they had duties toward him. Here are a few examples.

Husbands ought to love their wives as their own bodies. He who loves his wife loves himself.
—EPHESIANS 5:28

Husbands, love your wives and do not be harsh with them.
—COLOSSIANS 3:19

Fathers, do not exasperate your children; instead, bring them up in the training and instruction of the Lord.
—EPHESIANS 6:4

Masters, provide your slaves with what is right and fair, because you know that you also have a Master in heaven.
—COLOSSIANS 4:1

Slaves, obey your earthly masters with respect and fear, and with sincerity of heart, just as you would obey Christ.... And masters, treat your slaves in the same way. Do not threaten them, since you know that he who is both their Master and yours is in heaven, and there is no favoritism with him.
—EPHESIANS 6:5, 9

Women in Marriage

In Greek and Jewish society, one of the wife's roles was to be sexually available to her husband. She belonged to him and he owned rights to her sexually. But the reverse was not true; it was a society full of double standards. Men were not punished for having sex outside marriage, and many men had more than one wife. Paul, in his teaching on marriage, argues that the wife does not have authority over her own body, the man does. He continues, though, with this significant thought:

In the same way, the husband's body does not belong to him alone but also to his wife.

—1 Corinthians 7:4

In making this statement, Paul introduced a view of women's equality in marriage that was truly revolutionary. Never before had a woman been given a right over her husband's body.

Women in Ministry

Jewish teaching of the day implied that the significance and value of a woman was rooted in her roles as a wife and a mother. Paul, however, saw them not only as partners in their marriages but also in his ministry. Women joined with him in spreading the gospel, and some were significant leaders in their own local congregation. Paul commends the work of faithful and fruitful women in the church. In Romans 16:1–27, ten of the twenty-four people mentioned and honored are women. Some of the women that he praises are apostles, teachers, deaconesses, and businesswomen.

There are three passages of Scripture that were written by Paul that, on first reading, appear to indicate that he did not allow women to operate in some of the spiritual gifts or hold some positions of ministry. It is these scriptures that have been misinterpreted over the centuries, keeping people confused and women shackled. I do not want to write a theological interpretation of these passages. This has been done very accurately and thoroughly in other books, such as Cindy Jacob's *Women of Destiny*. However, there are a few comments I would like to make.

First, God's Word does not contradict itself. Throughout the Bible there is consistency of theme, purpose, and doctrine. A passage of Scripture, therefore, must always be interpreted within the context of the whole Bible. The question, then, that needs to be asked is, What was Paul's theological stance throughout the New Testament? Put simply, Paul held the belief that there was no partiality or favoritism between genders in regard to the spiritual gifts. We read in his letters to the different churches that he allowed both men and women to pray, prophesy, lead, and teach.

These three passages of Scripture that appear to be inconsistent with this theology reflect the pressure Paul felt to maintain order in the New Testament church. Paul lived and breathed his apostolic calling and was a great advocate of the church. He was highly motivated to see that the world would favorably regard the young church and that Christians would behave in a manner that gave no offense to "Jews, Greeks, or the church of God" (1 Cor. 10:32–33). It is for this reason that Paul had to address some issues about women who were acting inappropriately in a couple of the churches.

It is important to remember that in these passages Paul is writing in a particular time, and his letters are directed to certain people in specific churches. What was written then does not always apply now in our given period of history, place, and culture. Dwight Pratt surmises in the *International Standard Bible Encyclopedia*, "Therefore, he [Paul] wrote responses to the way specific problems should be handled in different churches. Some of his remarks do not have direct relevance to our day."[12]

In the tables below I have summarized what many have incorrectly interpreted from these three passages and then applied to all women and all churches for all time. It is this misinformation that has pervaded our churches for centuries and has kept women restricted. I have also written in the first column an outline of the original issue that prompted Paul to write these letters to the churches. In the third column there is a summary of the correct interpretation of the passages and their correct application for all of us today.

Passage 1: 1 Corinthians 11:2–16—Letter written to the church at Corinth

The Original Issue	Incorrect Interpretation	Correct Interpretation
Paul is writing to the Corinthian church because he was concerned about: • The manner in which the women were praying and prophesying. • Women removing their head covering. (Note: this was the only item of clothing that set them apart from the men.)	• Every man is the head of every woman. • A woman may only publicly pray or prophesy wearing a head covering.	• The husband is the head of his wife. • Any woman may pray or prophesy publicly as long as she behaves respectfully and appropriately in her marriage and in society. • Women must not try to be like men but remain true to their gender and to themselves.

Passage 2: 1 Corinthians 14:29–40—Letter written to the church at Corinth

The Original Issue	Incorrect Interpretation	Correct Interpretation
Paul is addressing the issue of maintaining peace and order and the appropriate use of spiritual gifts. Disorder was occurring because too many people were prophesying and some women were being disruptive.	• All women in all churches are to keep silent. They are not allowed to speak in church meetings (i.e. teach, preach, pray, prophesy)	• Women should not speak inappropriately in church services. • Women (and men) can pray, prophesy, teach, or preach as long as they do so reverently and orderly.

Passage 3: 1 Timothy 2:9–15—Letter written to Timothy and the church at Ephesus

The Original Issue	Incorrect Interpretation	Correct Interpretation
Some women in the church at Ephesus were dressing, behaving, speaking, and teaching inappropriately, thus bringing the church into disrepute.	• Women are not to teach in churches. • Women should only learn. • Women are not allowed to lead or have authority over any man.	• Women, especially those who lead and teach, must dress and behave appropriately and decently. • Women need to learn the truth so they will not teach or be swayed by false doctrine. • Don't allow women to teach who are domineering and unsubmissive in nature. • Do allow women to lead or teach if they live righteously and possess sound doctrine and knowledge of the Scriptures.

Applying Paul's Teaching to Us Today

Women in the New Testament experienced a new sense of worth and freedom because Jesus and Paul treated them with value and respect. For the first time ever women were being allowed to participate in church services and worship. This resulted in the women feeling liberated not only in a spiritual sense but also in other areas of their lives. As an expression of this newfound freedom, the women had begun removing their head coverings. They assumed that equality meant that they could behave and dress like the men. Paul did not approve of this because in the culture of that day the men and women both wore a simple tunic; it was only long hair or the head covering worn by the women that differentiated the sexes. This radical behavior was challenging the customs of the local culture, thus bringing the church into disrepute.

Paul's concern was that the church should maintain the distinctions between the sexes. In this way the respect of the community would be preserved. He wanted men to stay men and women to stay women! Paul was reaffirming that women should be proud of their gender and its differences. He believed that women needed to retain what distinguished them as women—their femininity and beauty. I believe Paul's message is that a woman is most powerful when she remains true to her gender and true to herself.

> *If a woman can only succeed by emulating men, I think it is a great loss and not a success. The aim is not only for a woman to succeed, but to keep her womanhood and let her womanhood influence society.*
> —SUZANNE BROGGER[13]

In Bible times the head covering was also worn by women to symbolize their respect toward their husbands and his headship. In our time and culture we no longer have to wear a headdress as a sign of submission; however, we still need to adopt the behavior. I believe women who have not embraced submission will not only disqualify themselves from being used and promoted by God but will also bring disrepute to their husbands and churches. As a pastor and itinerant minister, I have seen churches, male pastors, and husbands who are undermined by the behavior and attitude of disrespectful wives. Furthermore, I believe men are unable to rise to the fullness of their potential if they are not released and respected as the leader in their own home.

> *A wife of noble character is her husband's crown, but a disgraceful wife is like decay in his bones.*
> —PROVERBS 12:4

This scripture vividly reminds us that wives carry an extraordinary power to be a blessing or a curse in their husband's life. God never specifically tells wives that they must love their husbands. He does, however, instruct women to adopt two attitudes and actions in their marriage relationship. The first is to submit to their husband. The second is to respect him.

> *However, let each man of you [without exception] love his wife as [being in a sense] his very own self; and let the wife see that she respects and reverences her husband [that she notices him, regards him, honors him, prefers him, venerates, and esteems him; and that she defers to him, praises him, and loves and admires him exceedingly].*
>
> —EPHESIANS 5:33, AMP

God intensely dislikes the behavior of women when they are disrespectful and critical of their husbands. Respect is shown in many ways. It can be demonstrated in a wife's words, manner, attitude, and body language. A long time ago I wrote down this great quotation: "As marriage counselor and Bible teacher David Edward says, a man can stand any kind of criticism, whether it's deserved or not, as long as it doesn't come from his wife. But it doesn't matter how much praise he's receiving from others—if his wife is critical of him, he is being undermined."[14] When I see women rebuke, belittle, mock, or make unreasonable demands of their husbands, it literally makes me feel ill. This type of behavior brings a deep sense of humiliation and shame into the lives of men.

Let me share with you the example of two contrasting attitudes by two different women. Ironically, they were married to the same man. You can read about the story in the book of Esther.

Vashti was the wife of Xerxes, the king of Persia. In the third year of his reign, Xerxes held a huge celebration to display the full extent of his splendor, glory, and wealth. During one of the many banquets, Xerxes wanted to show off his very beautiful wife to the princes, nobles, and leaders of the land. So, he summoned Vashti to put on her royal crown and to parade before all the men. The queen refused, and the king became enraged. This denial by Vashti brazenly demonstrated to everyone that she neither honored nor respected her husband and her king. It was deemed by the elders of the land that this rebellious refusal had the potential to infiltrate every part of their society. As a consequence, Xerxes was advised to divorce Vashti and find a new wife.

This is a fascinating story because Vashti, in her attempt to promote women's rights, actually diminished them. Her decision probably, and perhaps justifiably, was a reaction against being Xerxes's prized possession, which he could exhibit at his every whim. However, because Vashti was queen, her attitude and her action had potentially far-reaching consequences: she not only humiliated her own husband but all men. A decree was sent throughout the kingdom that every man should be ruler over his own household. This story shows us that assertiveness should never be exercised at the expense of honor and respect. Later in the story you can read that the new queen, Esther, was able to beautifully and harmoniously combine these qualities. Her respect and admiration of Xerxes won her both favor and privilege.

The apostle Paul gives a timeless encouragement to wives, especially those who desire to be in prominent positions, to submit to and respect their husbands. Paul also raised a concern of which we must be mindful today: the issue of domineering women. In a number of the churches that Paul visited he encountered women who were overbearing, bossy, and abrasive. Throughout the years I have talked with many women who demonstrated a lack of respect towards their husbands or admitted to being "bossy control freaks." I am sure you have met women like this as well. They are opinionated, demanding, manipulative, and controlling. They are filled with an ugly spirit that reflects the worst of feminism. These women sometimes fight for position and power, but I believe in the long term God neither honors nor promotes domineering women.

If the Holy Spirit is tugging at your heart right now, perhaps you, too, are practicing these behaviors and attitudes. What must you do? First, you need to repent to God. Then you need to apologize to your husband. My encouragement would also be to seek counseling. The need to control is often an indicator of deeper underlying issues such as distrust, fear, or rejection. This type of behavior ultimately reveals an inability to obey God and to depend upon Him. Therefore, you need to make a decision to trust God, His Word, and His ways. I believe that when you make this decision, you will experience personal freedom and a happier marriage.

The aim of this chapter has been to provide a summary of the truth as recorded throughout the pages of the Bible regarding the roles, status, and value of women. I am convinced that when truth is not fully revealed, understood, and applied, it can lead to the adoption of inappropriate attitudes and actions. Truth is powerful, as it brings knowledge, wisdom, justice, and freedom. It is essential, therefore, that men and women are taught this truth. I'm sure you'll agree with me. It is impossible to do what we do not know!

Jesus said, "If you hold to my teaching, you are really my disciples. Then you will know the truth, and the truth will set you free."

—JOHN 8:31–32

TIME TO REFLECT

- What misinformation and misunderstandings prevail in your home, your church, and your community regarding the status, roles, and value of women?
- After reading this chapter, has the truth challenged or enlightened any confusion or ignorance that you may have held?
- What has been your understanding about headship and submission? Has this been confirmed or changed by the teaching in this chapter?
- If you are a wife, how do you apply the truth that you have been created to be your husband's helper?
- Do you have any respect or control issues in your life?

stepping up,
stepping out

Chapter Twelve

PREPARING FOR PROMOTION

In the quest to see ourselves rise, we must assume responsibility to be the type of woman that God would endorse. He does not want His church full of controlling, aggressive, and overbearing women. That's a scary thought! God wants women who are strong but not domineering, women who are assertive but not aggressive, women who are called but not competitive, women who'll partner but not contend with others. I want to challenge you today to make the choice to be a woman whom God would be pleased to promote.

There are traits we can have and things that we can do that will please God and capture His attention. When we embody these qualities, it is more likely that our heavenly Father will place His hand upon our lives. When He does, we will experience His favor, blessing, and promotion. In this chapter we are going to look at four qualities that bring delight to God's heart.

From heaven the LORD looks down and sees all mankind; from his dwelling place he watches all who live on earth—he who forms the hearts of all, who considers everything they do.... But the eyes of the LORD are on those who fear him, on those whose hope is in his unfailing love.
—PSALM 33:13–15, 18

QUALITY 1: CONSECRATED LIFE

Earlier in the book I highlighted the fact that on many occasions throughout this century God has prophetically declared that He is raising an army. This means that all Christian men and women are called to be soldiers in God's army and to advance His kingdom.

I have discovered two powerful truths about the life of a soldier:

- Truth 1: A soldier's life is not his or her own.
- Truth 2: A soldier fights for someone and something.

Many years ago I was at a conference in which my pastor, Phil Pringle, prophesied about the army of God. He said, "I am raising an army of holy women!"[1] This word *holy* pierced my spirit like a dagger. I wept and wept. I felt an incredible conviction to be holy and a burden to encourage other women to holy living.

A holy life is a consecrated life. *Consecration* means "set apart for sacred purposes." When you live a holy life, your life is wholly His. This means you have made a conscious decision to live for God, His purposes, and His will. You have chosen to follow God even when there is a cost to your own personal comfort, routines, and vision. A holy woman is like a soldier. She is someone who recognizes that her life is not her own; she lives for His higher purposes. If we are going to be holy women, we must place our lives on the sacrificial altar and say these words to Jesus: "I'm yours!"

> So here's what I want you to do, God helping you: Take your everyday, ordinary life—your sleeping, eating, going-to-work, and walking-around life—and place it before God as an offering.
> —ROMANS 12:1, THE MESSAGE

A consecrated woman has decided that Jesus is not only her Savior but also her Lord. She has allowed Jesus to be her Boss, her Master, and the one in control of her life. She has taken to heart these words of Jesus:

> "If anyone would come after me, she must deny herself and take up her cross daily and follow me. For whoever wants to save her life will lose it, but whoever wants to lose her life will save it."
> —LUKE 9:23–24, AUTHOR'S PARAPHRASE

As a holy woman, I have experienced the cost of following Jesus. There have been times when God has asked me and my family to do specific things. These requests have called for sacrifice and brought challenges into our world. For example, in the early 1990s we were called by God to plant a church in the Philippines. At that time we were a young married couple with a successful business, a new house, and a baby. However, we chose to obey God and follow His call to pack our bags and go live in a developing country. This meant leaving our family, friends, and home and selling our business.

Looking back, those years were probably some of the toughest of our lives. Apart from having to adapt to the different culture, we also experienced testing trials and intense spiritual warfare. I must say, however, that we never regretted it for a moment. We knew without a shadow of doubt we were in the right place doing the right thing at the right time. God had called us, and we chose to listen, follow, and obey Him.

I have learned that God's army is not built through conscription. You actually sign up by volunteering. It is totally our choice to serve the King of kings and His cause. My heart and my thoughts often resound with this statement:

It's not about what God can do for me but what I can do for God.

In my journey of following and serving God, there have been significant moments when I have consecrated my heart afresh to Him. Upon reflection, these times have often come just before a promotion in God. To me, consecration is the foundation upon which God is able to build my life. It all begins with consecration and how much I am prepared to lose my life and let Him be Lord. If I want to be used by God in significant and influential ways, I believe that the higher I dream, then the deeper I must dig to build these stronger foundations of a consecrated life.

QUALITY 2: PURITY OF HEART, CHARACTER, AND CONDUCT

Holiness is a multifaceted quality. It demands that we live wholly for Him but also that our lives are wholesome. A holy woman keeps her heart pure. Her life is above reproach. She is a woman of integrity. She is a woman who fears God. She keeps her attitudes and motives in check. Her speech and her conduct are measured. She is highly regarded by others. She lives a moral and upright life. She manages her home and loves her children. She loves God and serves Him.

Above all else, guard your heart, for it is the wellspring of life.
—PROVERBS 4:23

A holy woman establishes boundaries in her world. She is careful what she allows into and out of her heart. She is cautious what she reads and watches on television. She is not greedy for money, power, or prestige. She does not eat or drink excessively. She wisely chooses her friends and what she does with her time. She is not lazy or frivolous. She keeps her heart and eyes only for her husband. She is not overcome with anger or jealousy. She is kind and compassionate. She repents when she has sinned. She forgives when she has been wronged.

In 1 Timothy 3 and Titus 1 there are a list of attributes, such as the ones I have just mentioned, that must be met before a person can be placed into a position of oversight in the church. Interestingly, not one of these traits is a talent or a skill. They are all qualities focused on godly character and conduct. We must conclude, therefore, that when God is going to promote His daughters, He will select women who have chosen to live holy and righteous lives.

In the early part of the Bible, we read about the life of Miriam, who was Moses's sister. She was a fascinating woman because she embodied both strengths and weaknesses. We are first introduced to Miriam as a young girl watching over her baby brother while he floats in a basket down the Nile River (Exod. 2). This was an attempt by Moses's mother to save her son's life, because the Egyptian authorities had sent out an order that all Hebrew baby boys should be slaughtered. The princess of Egypt discovered the baby floating in the basket, and Miriam, who was playing nearby, resourcefully offered to find a wet nurse to feed the child. Coincidentally, this woman just happened to be Moses's own mother! In this story, Miriam showed both faithfulness and initiative, thus saving Moses's life.

Many years pass, and we meet Miriam again as an adult woman (Exod. 15). Moses by then had been appointed by God to deliver Israel from the oppressive rule of the Egyptians. Miriam wholeheartedly supported Moses as he lead the entire nation through the Red Sea toward the Promised Land. God had also gifted Miriam to be a prophetess, and in this role she showed remarkable leadership as she lead the nation in a joyful outburst of praise and worship. The people sang and danced in an expression of thankfulness to the almighty God who had miraculously redeemed them.

Sadly, the next encounter we have with Miriam is in Numbers 12, when she and her brother Aaron are complaining about Moses. Together they argued and questioned, "Has the Lord spoken only through Moses?...Hasn't he also spoken through us?" (v. 2). Miriam became fiercely jealous that her younger brother had been esteemed by God and the nation of Israel as a greater leader and prophet than herself.

God was so angered by Miriam and Aaron's disrespectful attitude that He took the three siblings aside to deal with the matter. God spoke strongly to them about how He had specifically chosen and appointed Moses to be the nation's leader and prophet. He explained that He not only spoke to Moses in dreams and visions but also face to face. As a consequence of Miriam's sin, she was stricken by God with leprosy. In those days, this disease was both a social disgrace and a death sentence. Moses cried out to God for mercy, and after one week Miriam was restored.

Miriam's life reminds us that we must fight to keep our heart, our character, and our conduct always pure before God. Miriam foolishly allowed pride and resentment to infiltrate her heart, poisoning her attitudes and her actions. We must remember some fundamental lessons that you and I will be tested on at some time in our lives:

- In our giftedness we must not become proud.
- In our success we must stay humble.
- In our calling we must not compare.
- In our service to our leaders we must stay loyal.

I am stirred by these words of David:

Search me, O God, and know my heart; test me and know my anxious thoughts. See if there is any offensive way in me, and lead me in the way everlasting.

—Psalm 139:23–24

QUALITY 3: COMMITMENT, FAITHFULNESS, AND LOYALTY

For the eyes of the LORD range throughout the earth to strengthen those whose hearts are fully committed to him.

—2 CHRONICLES 16:9

One of the character traits God regards highly is commitment. Committed people are loyal, trustworthy, and dedicated. They have pledged an allegiance to someone or something, and they remain faithful to that relationship or responsibility.

God is delighted when we show commitment to Him, to our leaders, to our spouses, and to the other people in our world. I have observed that the place where this quality of commitment is often tested is in our own home church with our own leaders.

Using the analogy again of the army, we can understand that soldiers are not meant to be lone rangers, fighting for themselves or by themselves. It is the same for Christians. Our effectiveness is minimized when we work alone. More is achieved when soldiers or believers work together toward a common cause. In any team situation it is necessary to have appointed leaders and a chain of command. A soldier in God's army must be loyal, possess a servant's heart, and be submitted to the leaders placed over them.

It is vital that we recognize how this affects us today. I have seen too many Christians who are highly gifted and have big dreams but are unwilling to commit themselves to a church or to a pastor. God has determined that our faith will operate in the context of a local church and under the leadership of a pastor. It is both our choice and responsibility to be committed to a church and its leaders. Our loyalty to them is a reflection of this attribute of commitment in our lives.

With this in mind I want to pose a question to you: Are you a member of one church and committed to the vision and authority of its leaders? If you could not answer yes to this question, I would encourage you to go no farther until you have changed this situation in your life. It is my belief that your call as a believer and your potential as an individual will only be fully released and realized when you place yourself under the authority and covering of a pastor and a church.

Let me ask you two further questions:

1. Do you use your gifts and time in some tangible way to help build the people or programs of your church?
2. Are you involved in an area of your church, but the pastor does not agree with your approach or attitude?

During the few decades that I have been in church, I have met two types of Christians who are hazardous to the health of any church. First, there are those who position themselves on the sideline, where they take on the role of a spectator or a critic. Second, there are those who do get involved, but they have their own agenda and thus undermine the vision and authority of the leaders over them. Both of these types of people lack the essential character trait of commitment. I have seen time and time again that God is unwilling and unable to bless and promote these people.

It is a common phenomenon that before God gives you your own vision, you must learn to serve someone else's. Before others show loyalty and faithfulness to you, you must demonstrate allegiance to others. Before God gives you people to lead, you must learn to follow. Before others work for you, you must learn to work for others. In the kingdom of God the requirements for promotion have always been and always will be a servant-hearted attitude, coupled with commitment, faithfulness, and loyalty. It is amazing how these attributes will capture the attention and favor of God.

Let love and faithfulness never leave you; bind them around your neck, write them on the tablet of your heart. Then you will win favor and a good name in the sight of God and man.

—PROVERBS 3:3–4

There are a number of women in the Bible who are noted for their character and their commitment. The one who stands out to me the most would have to be Ruth. She truly is an extraordinary woman. Her loyalty to her mother-in-law, Naomi, paved the way for God to honor her and bless her future. Naomi and Ruth found themselves widows living in a foreign land. This meant they were destitute, because without husbands or sons they had no financial support. Naomi chose to release her daughter-in-law to return to her own homeland and family, but Ruth refused, saying:

"Don't urge me to leave you or to turn back from you. Where you go I will go, and where you stay I will stay. Your people will be my people and your God my God. Where you die I will die, and there I will be buried. May the LORD *deal with me, be it ever so severely, if anything but death separates you and me."*

—RUTH 1:16–17

As a result of this decision, Ruth met a virtuous man by the name of Boaz. He was actually a relative of Naomi's, and according to the Hebrew law he was the one who could redeem Ruth's life by marrying her, which is exactly what happened. Ruth married Boaz, and together they produced a son, Obed. He went on to be the grandfather of King David and one of the ancestors of Jesus, the King of kings and the Lord of lords. It's amazing what blessing, honor, and promotion is on the other side of loyalty.

It is interesting to point out that before Boaz had ever met Ruth, he had already heard about her. Boaz said to Ruth, "All my fellow townsmen know that you are a woman of noble character" (Ruth 3:11). Whispers had gone around the community that Ruth was a hardworking woman of integrity who was totally committed to loving and caring for her mother-in-law. This is what you might call good gossip! Reputation is such a powerful thing. In this story, we see that a good reputation paved the way to Ruth's promotion.

Jesus said on a number of occasions in parables he taught the people:

"Well done, good and faithful servant! You have been faithful with a few things; I will put you in charge of many things."

—MATTHEW 25:21

Before promotion there is always a test to see if we will be faithful with the little things that God has placed in our hands. What are these little things?

They can be money, a resource, a responsibility, a person, a privilege, a task, a talent, or a spiritual gift. When we prove that we are wise and faithful stewards with these little things, then God will always give us more. More what? More money, resources, responsibilities, people, privileges, tasks, talents, and spiritual gifts! Let me encourage you, therefore, to be a woman who is faithfully committed to doing whatever God has asked you. If you do well today, God will be able to bless your tomorrow.

QUALITY 4: STRENGTH

She is clothed with strength and dignity.

—PROVERBS 31:25

Many years ago I studied the Proverbs 31 woman, and I remember placing my Bible to my heart and praying, "Lord, I want to be like this woman." Over the years, I have allowed this unnamed woman to be an inspiration and a role model for my life. I have hungered to be everything she is and everything she does. She has been my role model and my challenge to grow, mature, and rise as a woman of God.

A wife of noble character who can find? She is worth far more than rubies.

—PROVERBS 31:10

Many women do noble things, but you surpass them all.

—PROVERBS 31:29

In these two verses we read that this woman is noble, and she does noble things. This word *noble* is translated in different Bible versions as "good," "excellent," "worthy," or "virtuous." The original Hebrew word is *chayil*, and it has four different meanings. They are:

1. strength, might
2. ability, efficiency
3. wealth
4. force, army

The definitions of this word encapsulate the attributes of this amazing woman. Like a soldier in an army she is powerful, mighty, and forceful. As a woman of influence she is wealthy, efficient, and capable. There is one word, though, that best sums her up: *strong*.

Let's look at the different areas where the Proverbs 31 woman exhibits strength. We can allow her life to be an inspiration as we pursue our own personal growth.

Mentally Strong

This woman has the capacity to carry the load of many different responsibilities. She is a capable and competent person. She loves her family, manages a household, runs a number of businesses, and contributes to her community. In my life I constantly face the need to grow in capacity. With every new promotion in God there has been a stretching of my ability to cope and to carry yet another responsibility. I have found that my mental strength has often been limited by my own personal management skills. To increase my capacity, I have had to learn time management principles, such as keeping a diary, prioritizing, planning, and establishing routines and systems.

Emotionally Strong

I have never envisaged the Proverbs 31 woman being stressed, anxious, or emotionally unstable, despite her full and busy life. She is a woman of dignity. She has a strong sense of self and is peaceful and predictable in her manner. I have found that to grow in emotional strength I have had to do a number of things. To find wholeness for my wounded heart, I actively pursued a journey of emotional healing, which included seeking help from a counselor. A practice I also have implemented in my life is to process my emotions. I have discovered that it is not healthy to ignore them or pretend they don't exist, so I either write about my challenges in a journal or talk through them with a girlfriend or my husband. I have found that there is power and freedom in facing, understanding, and resolving my emotions. The third strategy has been to grow up and take responsibility for how I respond to the emotions that invade my heart. Sometimes a rational decision can shift an emotion that tries to overtake me.

Physically Strong

This woman is strong in stature and physically fit. She works long, hard days, and her arms are busy doing strenuous tasks. We need to be women who maintain our fitness through regular exercise, watching what we eat, and finding the balance of work and play. When our bodies are robust, then our stamina is strong. With greater endurance and energy levels we are able to achieve more in life.

Financially Strong

One of the qualities I passionately admire about the Proverbs 31 woman is her financial strength. She is a woman of wisdom when it comes to dealing with money. She is competent at managing money, making money, and multiplying money. She oversees the affairs of her household, clothing business, and investment properties. I love this woman's entrepreneurial talent. Not only is she a woman of vision but she has also learned the necessary, practical skills, such as book-keeping, budgeting, and business plans. Jesus clearly stated in a number of parables that when a person is faithful with money, this will lead to promotion in other areas of their life (Matt. 25:14–30; Luke 19:11–27). This is a great reason to learn the art of wise money management.

Relationally Strong

Something that really stands out to me about the Proverbs 31 lady is that she has strong and healthy relationships. Her husband and children love, appreciate, and honor her. She is a continual source of blessing to them. All day long she connects with people; and, she does this with wisdom, grace, and respect. She understands the principles that build relationships, such as generosity, honesty, loyalty, and integrity. She is adept at relating to people, whether they are her servants, neighbors, community elders, business colleagues, or the poor and needy.

Strong in Values

The Proverbs 31 woman builds her life on unshakeable values. She knows who she is, what she stands for, and what is important to her. I have found that people who don't have a strong personal philosophy get buffeted around by other people's perceptions, opinions, and beliefs. Furthermore, they are more likely to be tempted by the devil in areas of character and morality. I believe it is essential to spend time reflecting upon and defining what your own personal values and convictions are, because they will determine your decisions and actions, whether you are aware of it or not!

Strong in Vision

Whenever I read this poem, I am always challenged by the capacity of this woman to carry vision. I picture the Proverbs 31 woman at her spinning wheel: as she twists and pulls the yarn, her heart is leaping with wonderful dreams and wild ideas—the design of a new dress, the poor person down the road who needs help, the new merchant who will take her dresses across the seas, what her children will be like when they grow up, the best block of land to purchase, planting a vineyard…

I believe each one of us must be like her and take the time to dream and allow our imagination to visualize our future possibilities. I want you to catch this! The vision you carry today will be your future tomorrow.

From my experience, I have found that my readiness for promotion is often hindered by an area of weakness in my life. In a way, my personal limitations can become shackles I place around my own legs. I am often challenged by God to develop and strengthen an area in my world. When this happens, I actually have to allow God to challenge and stretch me. Then I do practical things that promote growth. I read books, set goals, change habits, and pursue personal disciplines. We are all on a journey of personal growth until the day we die. I believe that if you just keep growing, then you will keep moving forward.

Personal development is your springboard to personal excellence. Ongoing, continuous, non-stop personal development literally assures you that there is no limit to what you can accomplish.
—Brian Tracy[2]

TIME TO REFLECT

- Reflect on what it means:

  For your life to be consecrated to God.

  To give your whole life as an offering to God.

  To voluntarily commit to serve the King and His cause.

- Read through the qualities of character and conduct listed in 1 Timothy 3 and Titus 1 and rate yourself for each attribute.

- What is the level of loyalty and faithfulness you have toward your pastor and your church? How is this commitment demonstrated in your life?

- What are the "little" things that God has entrusted into your care?

- Answer this question regarding your reputation: If people were to talk about me, what would they be saying? If you are discussing this chapter with others, encourage one another by sharing the positive attributes of each person in the group.

- Which area of your life needs to be strengthened? Why? What are you going to do to bring change and growth in this area?

Chapter Thirteen

READY, SET, GO

And without faith it is impossible to please God.

—HEBREWS 11:6

If there's one attribute that will catch God's attention and bring a smile to His face, it would have to be our faith! He loves it when we believe and when we step out in faith. It was my desire to finish this book with an inspiring story of faith, so I have chosen the story of Jesus and Peter walking on water. It beautifully captures the spirit and the message of this book—to rise up and step out. Let's have a look at what happened.

> *Immediately Jesus made the disciples get into the boat and go on ahead of him to the other side, while he dismissed the crowd. After he had dismissed them, he went up on a mountainside by himself to pray. When evening came, he was there alone, but the boat was already a considerable distance from land, buffeted by the waves because the wind was against it. During the fourth watch of the night Jesus went out to them, walking on the lake. When the disciples saw him walking on the lake, they were terrified. "It's a ghost," they said, and cried out in fear. But Jesus immediately said to them: "Take courage! It is I. Don't be afraid." "Lord, if it's you," Peter replied, "tell me to come to you on the water." "Come," he said. Then Peter got down out of the boat, walked on the water and came toward Jesus. But when he saw the wind, he was afraid and, beginning to sink, cried out, "Lord, save me!" Immediately Jesus reached out his hand and caught him. "You of little faith," he said, "why did you doubt?" And when they climbed into the boat, the wind died down. Then those who were in the boat worshiped him, saying, "Truly you are the Son of God."*

—MATTHEW 14:22–33

Perhaps you have read this passage on many occasions but never took the time to let this story truly impact you and ignite your faith. Let's take a fresh look at this amazing feat. Jesus and Peter actually walked on water. Their faith enabled them to defy the natural laws of buoyancy and gravity. What an extraordinary exploit! It is my prayer today that you will catch their spirit of faith. I know this story can stir each of us to boldly believe that our faith can accomplish astounding things.

I am going to highlight five significant points from this story that we can apply to our own journey and steps of faith.

1. JESUS PREPARES THE WAY

It is my belief that Peter was able to walk on water because Jesus did so first. Jesus led the way by being an example and an inspiration. He showed Peter how to perform this miracle and then summoned him to follow.

It is the same with our life. We can rest assured that Jesus prepares and paves our way. The Bible says, "We are God's workmanship, created in Christ Jesus to do good works, which God prepared in advance for us to do" (Eph. 2:10). Every one of us has been created by God for a purpose and chosen by Him to carry out specific jobs. To understand this further, we can use the analogy that God has determined both the pathway of our life and the steps we must take. I get excited about this truth. Not only has God designed my purpose, but He is also coordinating opportunities by which my calling will be fulfilled. Let me give you an example from my own life.

Before I started my life coaching business, it brewed in my heart and mind for a number of years. During this time, I received a number of prophecies from people who were unaware of my thoughts and plans. The words they spoke were enormously encouraging because they confirmed what God was preparing both in me and for me. Here is a quote from one of these prophecies that you can take and apply to your own life: "'You didn't choose this path; I chose it for you,' says the Lord. 'I set you on it. I am still in the process of preparing you and positioning you.'"

I wrote in my journal, "I am on a path that God has set before me. He has put me on this path. He is leading and guiding me. He is not only preparing me but also preparing things for me to do. I am going through a process of being prepared and positioned. There are certain places, people, and positions in my future that God is preparing for me to influence. It is a process! I must walk through the process. I need to get ready for what God has gotten ready."

Here is an extract from another prophecy: "He has orchestrated this and is outworking this." I love the two key words that God selectively spoke: *orchestrated* and *outworked*. To *orchestrate* means to "devise, arrange, coordinate, plan, and organize." This is exactly what God does in our lives. He strategically sees and systematically plans the specific steps that we must walk. How wonderful it is to know that God is intricately involved in our lives. His hands, which lovingly created us, also lead and guide our daily lives. The word *outwork* implies that God will make it happen. He will make a way and He will do the work. God will open the doors, give you the ideas, provide the opportunities, and place the right people before you. Put simply, Jesus will prepare your way!

I want to point out, however, that we need to be careful not to fall into a trap of thinking God will do everything and that we can just sit back and watch our lives unfold. Yes, God has prepared the way for us, but we need to get ready. God has orchestrated the details, but we need to be obedient. God will 'outwork' the plan, but we need to take action. God has called, but we need to follow. God says, "Come," but we need to step out. Our Christian life is always a beautiful balance of God and us moving and working together.

This is what we see in this story. Peter walked on the water because Jesus prepared the way. Together they walked, and together they accomplished something extraordinary. Jesus was an example, an inspiration, and an encouragement. However, He did not piggyback Peter. Peter had to find his own courage, use his own faith, and take his own steps. Peter walked on the water with Jesus, but most significantly, he also walked on the water alone.

2. Jesus Calls, "Come"

I love what Jesus cried out to Peter: "Come" (Matt. 14:29). It was very simple and very direct. It challenged Peter not to stay still and not to remain the same. It was this one word that changed Peter's life, because it caused Peter to step out from all his comfort zones. He stepped out from the security of his peer group. He stepped out from the fear within his heart. He stepped out toward the terrifying ghost. He stepped out from the safety of the boat. And he stepped out to walk on the tumultuous water.

The call to arise and to shine is as simple and direct as the call to come. Jesus is standing before us and asking us to rise and be an influence in a dark and lost world. The question is, Will we heed the challenge? Will we step out of our own comfort zones? Will we be like Peter, who chose to respond to Jesus' call to come?

3. HAVE A GO!

The secret of getting ahead is getting started.[1]

I find it fascinating that Peter was the only man who overcame his fear, courageously believing that he could walk on water. The Scriptures say there were many disciples in the boat and that they were all terrified, yet Peter was the only one brave enough to have a go. Consequently, out of a possible group of twelve men, Peter was the only disciple who had the extraordinary experience of walking on the water with Jesus. This story greatly provokes me. I never want to be one of the people left watching in the boat. I want to be the one climbing out of the boat! What about you?

I am convinced that God waits for us to make bold decisions, to say, "Yes, I'm scared, but I'll have a go." Let's look again at the words from the story.

> *When the disciples saw him walking on the lake, they were terrified. "It's a ghost," they said, and cried out in fear. But Jesus immediately said to them: "Take courage! It is I. Don't be afraid." "Lord, if it's you," Peter replied, "tell me to come to you on the water."*
> —MATTHEW 14:26–28

The crucial ingredient Jesus knew the disciples needed was courage. That night the disciples were intimidated by many factors: the darkness, the turbulent waters, the ghostly appearance of Jesus, and the mere fact that someone was walking on the water. The words, "Take courage. It is I," were spoken by Jesus to all the disciples, but only Peter took hold of them.

To take courage is both a choice and an action. Courage is something you need to grasp hold of with your two hands. Then you put it on, like a piece of clothing. I often say to myself, "Until confidence is in me, I choose to put it on me." We can be heartened by the fact that we can access this courage, because Jesus is saying to you and me, "It is I." We need to remember that He is the one who is for us, with us, and in us. It is only Jesus who can give us the strength and power to be courageous.

Courage is always something that you apply to a specific situation. Let me ask you, then: "What is the area in your life where you need courage?"

- Has God asked you to do something new?
- Has He placed inside you an idea for a business?
- Is it time for a career change or a promotion?
- Do you have dreams that are yet unfulfilled?
- Is there a relationship that needs to be built?
- Is there someone you need to reach out to?
- Are you struggling and need help from a counselor?
- Do you need to address conflict in your relationships?
- Is there an area or job at your church where you need to be serving?
- Do you have desires or passions lying dormant in your heart?
- Do you have a talent that needs to be released or expressed?

Let me encourage you to pinpoint the area of your life where you need to take hold and put on courage. Everything you do that is new or stretching requires valor. Every step of faith means pushing beyond personal comfort zones. Courage is what we need in the face of intimidation. This is why we need to remember that Jesus is saying to you and me, "Come. Take courage. Rise up. Step out. Don't fear. Be brave. I have gone before you. I am with you. You can do it. Just have a go."

4. THE CONDITIONS WILL NEVER BE PERFECT

Don't wait until everything is just right. It will never be perfect. There will always be challenges, obstacles, and less-than-perfect conditions. So what. Get started now. With each step you take, you will grow stronger and stronger, more and more skilled, more and more self-confident and more and more successful.

—Mark Victor Hansen[2]

I'm not sure why, but as I was growing up I always envisaged Jesus walking on calm, still water. Often, when I see a crystal clear lake, I imagine walking on the top of it, just like Jesus. When writing this chapter and studying this story with fresh eyes, I was challenged by God to notice that Jesus actually walked on turbulent water. The conditions were rough and hazardous because the lake was being buffeted by strong winds. So Jesus and Peter walked not only on water but also over waves. This brings a totally different image to my mind and inspires my faith even more.

I believe many times in life we say to ourselves and our Father in heaven, "OK, I will do that when…" or, "Yes, God, I will step out if…" Many of us have a list of excuses or conditions that must be met before we will step out and be obedient. I have discovered that God never asks people to do something when the conditions in their life are favorable or when they're personally ready. It is important that we do not allow our own personal weaknesses—or the fact that we have a mortgage, a home, children, a career, or a business—to prevent us from being obedient and courageous. Our lives are rarely smooth and perfect. It is often in the midst of turmoil that God asks us to step out in a new way or to serve Him in a greater capacity. If Peter didn't allow the unfavorable conditions to be an excuse, neither should we!

As I am writing this chapter, I am reflecting upon the times when God has asked me to do something significant for Him. There has always been a cost and sacrifice involved. Never have I been ready or were the circumstances easy. When we left Australia to live in the Philippines, we gave up a business, a new house, our home church, friends, and extended family. We gave up white beaches, western food, privacy, disposable diapers, a prosperous income, a nice car, clean air, and a comfortable lifestyle. We walked into heat, humidity, hardships, loneliness, persecution, and trials. We adopted rice, "jeepney" travel, simple living, hand washing, cold showers, smoggy air, bustling traffic, and an unknown language. The conditions were definitely not perfect, either to leave Australia or to live in the Philippines. But that did not stop us.

When God stirred in me the need to write this book, I felt overwhelmed. Once again, the conditions were not smooth. I had only started my business three months earlier; it was still new and needing my attention. I was also juggling a full life with working another job, teaching at a Bible college, traveling with my husband, and at times speaking in other churches and conferences. I knew how much time, energy, and discipline would be required to write a book. I also had a suspicion that there would be some personal challenges I would encounter along the way (and there have been!). When I said, "Yes, God," I did so understanding the cost of what was involved.

I know a wonderful lady who has been saved for a number of years. One day she went to church, and the message that was preached challenged her greatly. She wrote these words to me in an e-mail:

Went to church on the weekend, first time in six weeks. Was looking for God to convict me of my lack of commitment of late and was looking for a message...as you do! Interesting that I was focused on receiving a message from God about how I could improve myself or fix myself. WOW! What an awesome message about each and every one of us getting out in the community and showing God through our own kind works. This was like a bolt of lightning. I mean, here is me always thinking that I am not ready, or not good enough, or not sorted, or haven't dealt with all my stuff, or haven't worked out my gifts, or my calling, and full of insecurities and problems and blah blah blah and so couldn't possibly offer anyone anything, but that is so not true. God spoke to me about it on Sunday. It's a bit like the Nike message—just do it.

My friend had caught the principle that we are never ready, nor are our circumstances. We can make all the excuses in the world and wait for favorable conditions, but God is asking you and me, Will you count the cost and serve me? Will you step out, even in the wind and the waves?

5. THE STEPS WILL ALWAYS REQUIRE FAITH

From the beginning to the end, Jesus and Peter's walk on water is a story of faith. Jesus had only three years to teach the principles of the kingdom of God, and one of the most important truths He taught was faith. Jesus taught a variety of people using a range of methods. He taught one-on-one, in groups, and to the crowds. He taught by reading the Scriptures and telling parables. But His most powerful teaching tool was His own life.

Jesus taught the disciples servanthood by humbly washing their feet, and He taught them faith by performing miracles. These miracles were many and varied. His faith raised people from the dead and turned water into wine. His faith fed the multitudes and healed all who were sick. His faith calmed a storm and killed a fruitless fig tree. Walking on water was just one more demonstration to the disciples of Jesus' faith in action.

Another fact I found fascinating when I studied this passage was that Jesus actually walked over three miles across the surface of the choppy lake. It wasn't just a few steps. To walk three miles on land takes about an hour. This is some miracle. No wonder the disciples were freaked out. After leaving Jesus on the shore, I'm sure they would not have thought they would be seeing Him again that evening. They believed He was on a mountain praying. Suddenly, in the middle of the night, they saw Jesus walking on the water toward them.

Jesus' walk of faith prompted Peter to follow in His master's footsteps. Peter's question, "Lord if it's you…tell me to come to you on the water" (Matt. 14:28), was actually a statement of faith. Peter followed these words of faith with actions of faith. He stepped down out of the boat and took his first steps. He then continued to walk toward Jesus. I believe that Peter kept his eyes fixed on Jesus. I believe that in his heart and mind he continually said these words to himself, "If Jesus can, I can."

Perhaps the wind became increasingly wild or the swell suddenly rose, but something made Peter's eyes wander to the wind and the waves. I was trying to imagine how this might have happened. Perhaps Peter walked from the boat with his eyes locked on Jesus' eyes. When he reached Jesus, he would have had to turn around to walk back toward the boat. At that point, Peter would not have been able to see the face of Jesus. As he turned, his eyes would have been looking at everything else around him. This shift in focus possibly caused the drop in Peter's faith and the sinking of his body into the water. When this happened, Peter immediately called out to Jesus, "Lord, save me!" (Matt. 14:30). Jesus responded beautifully by taking hold of Peter's hand, and together they finished the walk on the water back to the boat.

What do we learn from this lesson of faith? Most importantly, we learn that anything is possible with faith. Whatever is in your heart, whatever promises God has spoken, whatever dreams He has given you, they can all happen. All we have to do is believe—believe even when circumstances are contrary, believe even when it seems impossible, and believe even when we are scared. Then all we have to do is act. The Book of James challenges us that faith without works is dead (James 2:14–26). In this story we see Peter's faith alive and active. His belief motivated him to take steps of faith. Without these action steps Peter would never have walked on the water.

For about seven years I was involved in a women's group. Throughout these years we supported and shared our lives together: the highs, the lows, the disappointments, the challenges and the victories. At times we laughed together and at times we cried. One thing we always did was believe in and for each other. The lives and hearts of two of my friends in this group particularly inspire me. For many years they carried a promise spoken into their hearts by God, and they walked out and fought a journey of faith. As you read their stories below, you will notice that both of them were asked by God at a certain time to undertake a specific action of faith.

My friend Annie became a widow at the age of 38 when her husband died of bone marrow cancer. For the next twelve years she valiantly and success-fully raised her two children. She believed and held on to the promise that God would give her a new husband. After many years, God said to her, "Go and buy some material for your wedding dress." In obedience, she went and chose the material. It was, however, another few, long years before her promise would come to pass. During that time, God took Annie on a journey of purifying her heart and her faith. Then one day she met Alan, a wonderful Christian man who just happened to walk into her office at work. After a short time, there was much rejoicing because Annie, at the age of fifty, married her man. Her promise was fulfilled.

My friend Heidi was pregnant with her first child when it tragically died in her womb. She had to endure labor knowing her beautiful baby girl, Paris, had already passed away. For the next five years my friend held on to the promise that she would have another baby. She prayed, fasted, wept, fought, and trusted. There was even a point when she let the dream die. After a fourteen-day fast when Heidi cried out for the faith of God, the Lord spoke to her, "Prepare the room." In faith, Heidi and her husband, Mark, pulled out the old cot, cleaned it up, and put it back together. They went shopping for baby goods and turned their home gym into the baby's bedroom. After waiting for years, Heidi conceived her promised child only three months after this step of faith. Her faith journey, however, was not yet finished. She went into premature labor and gave birth to her baby at twenty-eight weeks. After a long and challenging stay in hospital, their beautiful son, Samuel, did come home and is now a beautiful little boy.

From these stories and the example of Peter, we are reminded that what we start in faith, we must finish in faith. Peter commenced his walk in faith but lost his faith midway because he became distracted and looked at the circumstances. Let me urge you today that whatever God is calling you to do, you need to start, continue, and complete it in faith.

If you do not stand firm in your faith, you will not stand at all.
—ISAIAH 7:9

As a child, my perception of this story was that Peter had failed because he sank. I thought he lacked faith. When God placed this story in my heart years later, I read it over and over again, and in the process my whole understanding and impression of Peter was changed. I began to see just how astonishingly courageous Peter was. This might sound odd, but I actually felt proud of Peter. What he did was extraordinary. None of the other disciples were brave enough to overcome their fears and follow Jesus in this way.

Peter was an astonishing success. He did it: he stepped out and walked on the water and the waves. He achieved something that was impossible.

Even when he did begin to sink, he wisely called out to the one who could lift him back up. Most importantly, he finished what he started. Peter was tremendously successful. And that is what you and I can be. All we have to do is courageously step out and have a go at it!

Let me remind you of two small, yet powerful words: *I can.*

I can do everything through him who gives me strength.

—PHILIPPIANS 4:13

And let me tell you, I believe in you. I believe you can! You can step out of the boat. You can step out of fear. You can push through demonic opposition. You can realize all of your potential. You can express your passions. You can be a woman of influence. You can perform miracles. You can do extraordinary exploits. Yes, my friend, you can do anything.

TIME TO REFLECT

- Looking over your life, what are some times when you can see that Jesus had prepared your way? How do you think He is preparing your future?
- Using the analogy of the paths and steps, draw a picture of where God has brought you from and where He is leading you to.
- If Jesus is calling, "Come," how does this apply to you?
- In which area or areas of your life do you need to put on courage?
- What is your boat? Define the personal and situational comfort zones that could stop you from stepping out and obeying God.
- Is God asking you to perform a specific action of faith? Has He in the past?
- Finish this sentence: "I can _____."

Final Words

I'M CHEERING YOU ON

On every occasion I teach, give a talk, or preach a message, I always take the time to think about what I want my students or listeners to learn. I like to see in my heart and my mind the revelation they will catch and how this will impact their lives. Beforehand I pray and believe that every individual, in some way, will be different because of the words I will speak. Sometimes I even carry the people and the message in my heart. Like an intercessory, prophetic burden, this intense feeling is only released once I have delivered the message. I have gone through a very similar process and experience while writing this book. Let me share with you what I have been carrying, seeing, and believing for you.

I have desired for this book to inspire you afresh about God's mission for this planet and your purpose in advancing His kingdom. I have prayed that you would catch a spirit of courage so you will fulfill the call of God in your life. I have been motivated to see that all of your potential is released. I have longed for you to be set free and for you to know that you were created with a unique identity and purpose. I have desired that you would understand that you are a woman of influence who can make a difference. I have carried a burden that you will be stirred to rise up and step out in each and every area of your life.

I have already seen the people on the other side of you rising up. I see people who have been loved and blessed, people who have been healed and set free. I see you seizing opportunities to make new friends and be influential in the places where God has positioned you. I see people meeting Jesus and being miraculously healed. I see new businesses being birthed and job promotions being attained. I see happier husbands and stronger marriages. I see confident women walking tall and strong. I see women unswayed by insecurity and intimidation. I see women being recognized, raised, and released in their churches. I see women's lights shining bolder and brighter. I see women stepping up and stepping out. I see women impacting and influencing others.

I see women rising!

I also see the army marching and the river roaring. I see men and women powerfully partnering together. I see Christians carrying the presence of God into every street, home, and workplace. I see darkness pushed back and pure, radiant light beaming. I see the devil defeated and the name of Jesus lifted high. I see the church rising in every city and nation. I see the name of Jesus exalted and His glory covering all the Earth.

So, friend, my desire, my dream, and my burden is that this book has in some way transformed your life. My prayer is that you will know that you can have a powerful impact in this world, that you can make a difference because you are a woman of influence. All you have to do is get up and get going.

I'm cheering you on.

NOTES

CHAPTER ONE

1. Information about Joan of Arc has been taken from the following sources: Wikipedia Online Dictionary, http://en.wikipedia.org/wiki/Joan_of_Arc (accessed December 10, 2009), s.v. "Joan of Arc;" "Joan of Arc," Gale Cengage Learning, http://www.gale.cengage.com/free_resources/whm/bio/joan_of_arc.htm (accessed December 10, 2009); "Facts About Joan of Arc," Buzzle.com, http://www.buzzle.com/articles/facts-about-joan-of-arc.html (accessed December 10, 2009); "Joan of Arc," Discover France, http://www.discoverfrance.net/France/History/Joan_of_Arc.shtml (accessed December 10, 2009).

2. Information about Henrieta Mears has been taken from the following sources: Joyce Vollmer Brown, *Courageous Christians* (Chicago: Moody Press, 2000), 119–120; Wikipedia Online Dictionary, http://en.wikipedia.org/wiki/Henrietta_Mears (accessed December 10, 2009), s.v. "Henrietta Mears;" Dr. Waylon B. Moore, "Henrietta Mears," Mentoring, http://www.mentoring-disciples.org/mears.html (accessed December 10, 2009); "Henrietta Mears," *Historical Renewal*, http://www.historicalrenewal.com/biographies/bio_HMears.htm (accessed December 10, 2009).

3. Billy Graham, quoted in Dr. Waylon B. Moore, "Henrietta Mears," *Mentoring*, http://www.mentoring-disciples.org/mears.html (accessed December 2, 2009).

4. Information about Mother Teresa has been taken from the following sources: Wikipedia Online Dictionary, http://en.wikipedia.org/wiki/Mother_Teresa (accessed December 10, 2009), s.v. "Mother Teresa;" "Mother Teresa," NobelPrize.org, http://nobelprize.org/nobel_prizes/peace/laureates/1979/teresa-bio.html (accessed December 10, 2009).

5. Elizabeth George, *Beautiful in God's Eyes* (Eugene, OR: Harvest House Publishers, 1998), 171.

6. Christine Caine, "The Brave," C3 Everywoman Conference, October 28, 2006, C3 Oxford Falls, Sydney, Australia.

7. W. E. B. DuBois quote accessed at *Bella Online*, http://www.bellaonline.com/articles/art13565.asp (December 2, 2009).

Chapter Two

1. *Encarta World English Dictionary*, Microsoft Corporation, 2009, accessed at http://encarta.msn.com/encnet/features/dictionary/DictionaryResults.asp x?lextype=3&search=pillar, s.v. "pillar."

2. Wikipedia Online Dictionary, http://en.wikipedia.org/wiki/ Erechtheum, s.v. "Erechtheum."

3. Wedgwood advertisement printed in *Vogue Entertaining Guide*, October/November 1992, 11.

4. "Commissioned Officer," U.S. Army Web site, http://www.goarmy. com/about/officer.jsp (accessed December 2, 2009).

Chapter Four

1. Bob Briner, *Roaring Lambs* (Nashville, TN: Zondervan, 1993), http:// www.epiphanyresources.com/9to5/articles/roaringlambs.htm (accessed December 2, 2009).

2. Ibid.

3. Che Ahn, *Ministry Today*, May/June, 2006.

Chapter Five

1. Pope John XXIII quote accessed at ThinkExist.com, http://thinkexist. com/quotation/consult_not_your_fears_but_your_hopes_and_your/8220. html (December 2, 2009).

Chapter Six

1. Costa Mitchell, *Learn to Love Yourself* (Kwazulu-Natal, South Africa: Vineyard Publications, 1991), 45.

2. Ibid., 24.

Chapter Seven

1. Abraham Maslow quote accessed at "Quotes About Self-Actualization," *Gaia Community,* http://quotes.gaia.com/topics/self-actualization (December 2, 2009).

2. Marianne Williamson quote accessed at http://www.marianne.com (December 2, 2009).

3. Betty Bender quote accessed at "Betty Bender," Answers.com, http://www.answers.com/topic/bender-betty (December 2, 2009).

4. Susan Jeffers quote accessed at http://talentdevelop.com/fear2.html (December 2, 2009).

5. Lisa Jiminez, "Be Willing to Be a Little Outrageous to Get What You Want!," R-X Success, Inc., http://rx-success.com/artman/publish/article_2.shtml (accessed December 2, 2009).

6. Simone Weil quote accessed at "Simone Weil," PBS.org, http://www.pbs.org/wgbh/questionofgod/voices/weil.html (December 2, 2009).

7. Chuck Gallozi, "Understanding Fear," Personal-Development.com, http://www.personal-development.com/chuck/fear.htm (accessed December 2, 2009).

Chapter Eight

1. Mary Robinson, quoted in Helen Exley, *In Celebration of Women* (Exley Publications, 1996).

2. Wikipedia Online Dictionary, http://en.wikipedia.org/wiki/Fourth_World_Conference_on_Women (accessed December 2, 2009), s.v. "Fourth World Conference on Women."

3. "We've Come a Long Way Baby," *The Australian Women's Weekly,* October, 2003.

4. "The Good Wife's Guide," *Housekeeping Monthly,* May 1955.

5. Ed Silvoso, *Women: God's Secret Weapon* (California: Regal Books, 2001), 17.

6. Ibid., 96, 46–47.

7. Advisory Committee on Equal Opportunities of Women and Men, presented to Parliamentary Assembly at the Council of Europe, April 2004, http://assembly.coe.int/Documents/WorkingDocs/doc05/EDOC10643.htm (accessed December 2, 2009).

8. Martin Luther King Jr., "I Have a Dream," accessed at American Rhetoric Top 100 Speeches, http://www.americanrhetoric.com/speeches/mlkihaveadream.htm (December 2, 2009).

CHAPTER ELEVEN

1. Adam Clarke, *Adam Clarke Commentary on the Bible*, accessed at http://www.godrules.net/library/clarke/clarkegen2.htm (December 2, 2009).

2. Matthew Henry, *Matthew Henry's Commentary on the Bible*, accessed at http://eword.gospelcom.net/comments/genesis/mh/genesis2.htm (December 2, 2009).

3. Dwight Pratt, *International Standard Bible Encyclopedia*, accessed at http://www.bible-history.com/isbe/W/WOMAN/ (December 2, 2009).

4. Sue and Larry Richards, *Every Woman in the Bible* (Nashville, TN: Thomas Nelson Publishers, 1999), 219.

5. John Finkelde, *Created for Partnership* (Australia: Finkelde Ministries, 1996), 26.

6. Richards, Every Woman in the Bible, 7.

7. Ibid., 63.

8. Ibid., 204.

9. Finkelde, *Created for Partnership*, 13.

10. Ibid., 12–13.

11. Ibid., 18.

12. Pratt, *International Standard Bible Encyclopedia*.

13. Exley, *In Celebration of Women*.

14. Source unknown.

CHAPTER TWELVE

1. Phil Pringle, Oz Fire Conference, December 28, 2001, C3 Oxford Falls, Sydney, Australia.

2. Brian Tracy quote accessed at "Brian Tracy Quotations," compiled by Simran Khurana, About.com, http://quotations.about.com/od/stillmorefamouspeople/a/BrianTracy1_3.htm (December 2, 2009).

Chapter Thirteen

1. Quote accessed at ThinkExist.com, http://www.en.thinkexist.com/quotation/the_secret_of_getting_ahead_is_getting_started/8307.html (December 2, 2009).

2. Mark Victor Hansen quote accessed at "Mark Victor Hansen Quotes," ThinkExist.com, http://thinkexist.com/quotation/don-t_wait_until_every-thing_is_just_right-it_will/295163.html (December 2, 2009).

ABOUT THE AUTHOR

Amanda lives on the beautiful northern beaches of Sydney, Australia, with her husband, Patrick, and their two children, Jacinta and Tyler. For more than twenty years her church home has been C3 Church (formerly Christian City Church), Oxford Falls, where she is on the pastoral team and is a trainer at the C3 College. Amanda lectures on a variety of subjects, including management principles, money and wealth, proverbs, ministry gifts, and women living life well. She lived for two years in the Philippines, where she and her husband established a C3 church. They are now involved in planting and overseeing C3 churches throughout Asia and Africa.

In recent years Amanda has addressed conferences, colleges, churches, and business meetings both nationally and internationally. As a speaker, you will discover that Amanda is vivacious, sincere, and natural. She speaks with a prophetic edge and shares from her own life experiences. Her passion is to see lives changed.

Amanda and her husband have established four successful businesses. In 2006, Amanda began her own life coaching business, Your Café Coach. In her role as a life coach, she helps people fulfill their potential, pursue their dreams, and achieve their goals. She coaches local Sydney clients face to face at cafés; those who live elsewhere (nationally and internationally) she coaches over the phone or via the Internet.

LIFE COACHING AND SPEAKING

Amanda is available to speak at conferences, colleges, churches, and business meetings. She also coaches individuals or groups—in person if you live in Sydney, Australia, and by telephone or Skype if you live in other parts of Australia or overseas.

If you would like to discuss Amanda's availability for coaching or speaking or to find out further information go to: www.amandaantcliff.com or e-mail her at amanda@yourcafecoach.com.au.